How to Love Yourself: The Art of Loving Myself

Self Love as the Basis of High Self Esteem, Self Worth and Self Respect. Be Yourself and Love Yourself Right NOW.

JONATHAN KISLEV

Published in the United States by Goldsmith Press LLC.

Editor: Tania von-Ljeshk
Cover photograph: Scott Durham
Profile photograph: Doug Ellis Photography
Cover design: Slava "Inkjet" Noh

Praise for *How to Love Yourself: The Art of Loving Myself*

"For those who generally loathe the self-help genre, Kis-Lev's book is a breath of fresh air. Kis-Lev takes an orderly, methodical approach to finding affection for himself. And you can't not fall in love with him on the way."

— Laila Hoja, The Book Reviewer

"Practical and never preachy... Gave me many practical ideas, some of which I use ever since. The analysis of our brain-chatter patterns was absolutely brilliant."

— Daily Preacher

"Packed with fascinating insights about the reasons why we tend to put ourselves last on our list, this book will show you how to do otherwise. I only wish I had read it earlier."

— Alison Kahn, Peace For The Future

"Wonderful. . . . Kis-Lev shows how you can be happier with who you are, starting right now, with small, actionable steps accessible to everyone."

— Dr. John Vitals

"Kis-Lev exudes warmth from every page. As you read it you'll be inspired by his emotional confessions and liberating wisdom."

— Aven K. Lint, author and speaker

"Enjoyable and witty... The book is filled with the best quotes you'll ever find about the subject of loving yourself."

— Daniel J. Okla, The Jewish Daily

"Kis-Lev ("My Quest for Peace") brings a fun, sensitive verve to now well-tread self-help tropes... The tone is far more feisty than academic, and there's humor on every page, all of which is exactly what his intended audience most needs..."

— The Monthly YOU Reader

"If touchy-feely self-help tomes make you feel less than inspired, this no-nonsense manifesto to self-love might be just what you're looking for. Jonathan has a gift for writing in a very digestible way that will appeal to everyone."

— Dan Klein, The Last Opinion

"The Art of Loving Myself will silence your inner critic and help you build a life worth living. You will find practical and easy ways to connect with your inner self and improve your life dramatically."

— Joan Kelvin, author The Secret Inside

"Author and artist Jonathan Kis-Lev takes the self-help book to another level with his cutthroat humor and in-your-face honesty. The short, well-written chapters fly away quickly. Too quickly…!"

— Janice Kline, speaker and author

"Kis-Lev has probably written the most moving self-help book many readers will ever get their hands on… Now you have permission to upsize your serving of love to yourself. Enough with the crumbs!"

— Bill T. Harry, Harry Books

"Moving and riveting… Reading this book was like talking to a best friend – the one that will tell you like it is no matter the circumstances and that forces you to think outside the box."

— Maria Velázquez, coach and trainer

"I cried and laughed… This guide will make you feel like it actually is okay to put yourself first… inspiring!"

— Jo Levi, The Reviewer

"Kis-Lev has turned his own pain and traumas into a source of wisdom and comfort for the rest of us. Brilliant."

— Mira Hudson, *The Life of Mira*

"Empowering… If you need to see an example of vulnerability done well, just read the work of Jonathan Kis-Lev."

— Nadia Joels, The Bookreview Club

"An enlightening, laugh-aloud read. . . . Filled with open, honest glimpses into Jonathan's real life, woven together with constant doses of humor and wisdom."

— Jane Silva, author and columnist

To all of my friends around the world. This book is for you. Thank you for encouraging me to be myself. This book is my tribute to all of you.

- J. K.

INTRODUCTION

This book you are holding is a book full of love. It was written with love, with the hope that it will reach you wherever you are, touch you and inspire you.

In many ways I've been writing this book for years. I've been on the journey of choosing to love myself for many years now. The past five years I've dedicated myself wholly to the subject. I've read books, I've gone to seminars, and I practiced various exercises regularly.

You may ask why this obsession with this subject of loving yourself?

Quite frankly, I don't know. All I know is that I have felt a hunger to fill a gap in my soul. I've tried to fill it with work and accomplishments. And it didn't work. I tried to fill it with love, romance and sex, and became even more depressed. I tried creation – doing art and writing – and it got me closer, but didn't fill the gap wholly.

I am a pleaser. I always liked to please others. I also liked to be well regarded. Early on I learnt that when I brought good grades home, I received positive attention and love. I therefore tried to bring the best grades I could. After school I did it with my work as an artist: bigger paintings, better paintings, more extravagant exhibitions – all to get positive attention. All to make me feel that I'm alright.

But soon enough this way of life took its toll. I was living for other people. I was trying to make my parents proud, my girlfriend proud, my siblings, friends, even distant acquaintances. And it was tiring, exhausting, and unhealthy.

I began having severe back pains, often paralyzing me for days. I did physiotherapy, acupuncture, whatever – it didn't help. And things were getting worse.

In my love life, I found myself in the second, if not third, unhealthy relationship. I was trying to be the good guy all the time, while not really knowing who I was and what *I* wanted. Even asking this question seemed to me like an odd, if not a rude, question to ask.

This book details my journey. It is a journey towards loving myself.

Have I arrived? Well, I think I'm still working on it. Each month, each year, I feel that I do love myself more. I feel that I respect myself more. Each year I'm becoming kinder to myself.

This journey has not been easy. To an extent, it still continues. I still have lots of work to do.

But the benefits I'm already ripping are amazing. So amazing, in fact, that I decided to sit down and write this book, to tell you all what's possible if you dedicate yourself to this journey.

Loving yourself, I found, is a form of art. And while I do not strive for perfection, I do appreciate those artists and artisans that have made their art a sublime one.

In this book I share the processes, the exercises, the mental highs and lows, and through personal example, I hope to inspire you to practice the art of loving yourself.

"I am an artist at living -
my work of art is my life."

—Daisetsu Teitaro Suzuki
Japanese Zen master and author

"If a man writes a book, let him set down only what he knows. I have guesses enough of my own."

—Johann Wolfgang von Goethe
19th century German writer and statesman

EXPERIENCE, NOTHING BUT EXPERIENCE

All I am about to share with you is my knowledge the way I experienced it, the way I came to understand it through being involved.

Much of it I learnt the tough way.

Don't get me wrong. I'm still working on this very thing myself. I am working on loving myself. On accepting myself for who I am.

It's a journey.

And I don't wait until it will be over.

Rather, each year I feel that I love myself more. I feel that I allow myself to giggle and laugh out loud, without caring all too much what others around me think. I allow myself to cry, or at least be vulnerable, around people I care about. I allow myself to seem stupid at times, asking questions for answers I think I should have known.

There is great freedom in being yourself. We all

love and are attracted to people that are just "themselves." Oprah Winfrey is an example. She is pretty good at being herself, and that's what makes me like her so much. So are other teachers and celebrities, when I sense that they are authentic and real, I love them all the more.

But the road to authenticity passes through self-love-town. You gotta be willing to accept yourself for who you are. Actually, more than accept - embrace.

I went to this Jack Canfield workshop in 2011, and he gave us this exercise of every evening standing in front of the mirror, and telling ourselves encouraging words. These would be words about how well you did that day, and stuff like that. No reprimand allowed. Oh, and yes, that end piece. He told us to, at the end, look ourselves in the eye and say, "I love you."

Arrrrrghhhhh!!!

I hated that.

I barely looked at myself in the eyes when I said that.

And when I did, I actually faked it.

It was as if I looked at someone I'd rather not be around, and say, "so nice to see you!"

Uh huh. Right.

Long way to go!

But I kept doing this darn exercise. Each night. Almost every night.

For months and months.

At the time, I was in an amazing relationship with a girl I thought I was to marry. I didn't want to embarrass myself by telling her that I do this weird mirror thing.

So I didn't.

I also didn't tell her other things that were showing up. I felt... I felt that she was judging me.

She wasn't the only one. I was judging myself constantly as well.

She used to – let's call her Autumn, that's a nice name – well, Autumn used to often be upset with me. It might have been something I said or did, she would retreat to her taking "space" and needing to be alone.

And so I was left being in a relationship, alone.

I also spoke to her about marriage, and about our future together. She was not into it. And she said that, and I'm paraphrasing, "given some things I've seen about you, about your inner insecurities, I just don't... see... myself marrying to such a person, you see?"

I nodded.

But I didn't see.

All I saw was how through me showing her my real self, my vulnerable self, I was actually pushing her away.

Was there something really that bad about me? To the core? That bad that Autumn could see and be... appalled by?

I wanted to quit this stupid exercise, that mirror

thing. I kept repeating some affirmative words to myself, and at the end telling myself that 'I love myself'. But I wasn't really there.

Deep inside I probably thought, "I love myself, BUT…"

And then the list would come.

"But you are too sensitive sometimes. But you are too stressed some times. But you are too girly some times. And sometimes, you're just plain annoying."

I can't even write these words right now. So much self-loathing, so much unaccepting of myself. I was far from embracing myself.

I went on with the mirror exercise. And following the encouragement of Autumn, I began going to a shrink. This psychologist was a friend of her psychologist. And so, for the first time in my life I began going to an actual, official therapy. I put my pride aside, and did everything I thought I needed to do in order to be able to save this relationship.

What was unique, though, was that Eyal, the therapist, actually was often upset with my stories about Autumn.

He'd say, "But did you tell her that it upset you that she did that?"

"I… tried…?" I said.

"Well, you should be able to communicate with her freely!"

So I tried. Every few weeks or so I mustered the courage and I would tell her. About her not accepting me. About her being easily hurt and forgetting who I am and that I love her. About her distancing herself from me. About me not knowing how to communicate with her.

We both had much work to do, I realize now.

Each time I finally spoke, Autumn would be all loving and embracing. I think it touched her, that I opened up, that I cared. That I cried.

But unfortunately, this feeling of openness within her lasted only a day or so. Then I'd get an SMS from her saying, "It was a bit much for me. I need to take some space."

I came to despise this word. "Space." What the heck.

In the beginning I used to give her all the "SPACE" I could. But after few days I felt that I was pretty lonely. What was this relationship for, if we can't connect and support, and be together?

Eyal would listen to me, explaining of how she needs some space now. I would see his eyebrows frowning, and his head shaking 'no'.

"But," he'd say, "every time you're trying to talk and solve things, she walks away."

"Yeah," I'd say.

The mirror exercise kept repeating. I began feeling a difficulty doing it. I hated it. I also hated the fact I was in a relationship that didn't work for me.

"I deserve better!" I said.

Eyal looked at me. Do I see a tinge of hope in his eyes?

"You do," he said.

"I can't stand how each time it's just 'sorry, this was too much for me,' and that then she's gone."

Eyal said, "Well, we are not judging Autumn. She has her own things to go through, and her places to grow. But we care about Jonathan, and it seems like you are torturing yourself."

"Yeah...?"

"Yes."

And so, few months later, with the help of Autumn's psychologist's psychologist friend, I dared to end it.

Autumn was outraged.

I was too.

Lots of tears.

I remember being by the sea, walking barefoot, feeling helpless. This relationship was supposed to be it. Like, IT it. And now I'm... alone? Again?

And Autumn was everything I could hope for. She was a freaking dancer, of national level, and a voracious reader, and a super intelligent girl, funny, charming.

But it just didn't sit right with me being on a journey of choosing ME. Of choosing myself, of choosing to treat myself well.

Autumn was echoing my past – me shunning parts of myself and not taking me for what I am, my WHOLE self.

Autumn was sweet. She meant well.

And Autumn eventually forced me to prove myself that I actually DO love myself.

There were rough months ahead. I kept doing the mirror exercise. At one point I might have added an actual hug, an embrace, of me rapping my arms around myself, tilting my head gently on my shoulder, and rocking myself from side to side. Few seconds of bliss, of care, of affection to myself.

Oh, how much I needed that.

With time there was more love to myself. I felt more… is dignified the word? I felt respect to myself. I felt like I had something to offer the world. Something to offer to a girl, a woman, that would be willing to die for me. Not 'die' die, but close enough.

With time I felt more respect and affection to myself.

About a year later I entered into a relationship with this girl, who was somewhat into it, somewhat not. For several dates and so she kept going back and forth. I was willing to be patient, I liked her a lot.

But I also liked myself a lot.

There was one time in which this new girl did something annoying, don't remember exactly what it was. She was probably short tempered about something rather. And in the way she spoke to me I felt like I was in that old movie again.

Darn it.

I hurried to say, before I regret, before I overthink it. "Hey, that... that wasn't... that didn't feel very nice. I'd rather you not speak that way to me. If you are upset, then say that, but don't... You know?"

And I saw something responding in her eyes, her demeanor changed. "Why, sure. You're right," she said.

I felt like such a MAN at that moment. No. I was not going to take any form of abuse- even the slightest. And I really really liked the way she responded.

I also felt that she liked the fact I said something. She later on embraced me closer. And a year or so later told me it was a defining moment for her. "It meant," she explained, "that you SEE me. That you really cared about my wellbeing."

I was a little dumbfounded of how it showed that, but I didn't complain.

Two more years later we got married. And that whole happily ever after thing.

Had I not had the courage to speak up for myself, we most likely wouldn't have been together today. Had I not did the mirror exercise religiously, including actually physically embracing myself, I wouldn't have had the courage to speak up. Had I not been determined to LOVE myself, I wouldn't have had the tenacity and the audacity to actually do this ridiculous mirror thing.

So my point is, CHOOSE YOU. Choose yourself. Love yourself. Work on giving more respect and more appreciation to yourself. Please?

"When I was around 18, I looked in the mirror and said, 'You're either going to love yourself or hate yourself.' And I decided to love myself. That changed a lot of things."

—Queen Latifah
American rapper and actress

"It sounds like a cliché but I also learnt that you're not going to fall for the right person until you really love yourself and feel good about how you are."

—Emma Watson
British actress and activist

MY REQUEST

My request from you is that you do love yourself. You have invested the time to read this. The money, the energy. I request, no, I demand from you, to love yourself.

Now, while it's a journey with many perks and future benefits, it ain't easy.

Yes, I don't want you to be misguided. Easy it ISN'T.

But it's an important journey nevertheless.

I ask you to take the time and ask yourself, daily: "If I really really truly loved myself, what would I do today? How will my day be different?"

You got to ask this question daily.

You also got to ask yourself, "Which kind of example do I give to others as to how to treat me?"

This means, if you are tired and exhausted, you tell

others, "please tire me and exhaust me!"

If you are burdened and upset, you tell others, "please burden me and upset me!"

If you feel rejuvenated and loved, you tell others, "please rejuvenate me and love me."

If you do one more favor for someone without really wanting to do it, you say, "please give me one more favor for me to do for you." And you and I know that it's always just one more thing, just one more favor. Your life is filled with 'just one more', that have accumulated to mountains of 'just one more's.

Now, it won't necessarily be easy. People like you the way you are. People don't like changes, and neither do you nor I. We hate changes. We are habitual people. Tell us where our cheese is, and leave us alone. Oh, it's a new cheese? Better? Neh, give me the old one, I'm already used to it.

So you will find that other people are used to a very very specific version of you.

The upgraded version of you? Well, no thanks.

People, especially those around you, will find that you are changing, and not for the better.

You are a pleaser. Yeah. I unmasked you! Why do you think you are reading this freakin' book?

Yep. That's what you are. You wanna be liked, and that is often more important than your sleep, than your time to yourself, than your healthy diet, than your hobbies and your indulges. You want to make others happy.

Now, why am I on your case?

Well, if you want me to get off your case, than quit reading.

The fact you keep reading is that you want me to preach you the gospel of relearning how to BE. You have conditioned yourself to act in a way that is harmful for you. It really is. I'm sorry, but it is.

There is a place inside you, a real place, of self-protection. This place, this guardian angel of sorts, has guided you here. To hear these words.

This place is telling you: if you won't slow down and begin treating yourself nicer – if you won't begin to put yourself first – if you won't start slowing down and showing love to yourself – then… well, things are gonna get bad.

Yep. I'm sorry again to be the messenger of bad news. But basically, what I'm gathering is that you are telling me to tell you that if you won't change, and ASAP, that means YESTERDAY, then things are going to begin surfacing.

Oh, I hate to tell you that. Like you, I'm a pleaser too. So, for me to tell you the bad news is NOT an easy thing.

But what I'm instructed to tell you is that all kinds of health issues, relationship messes, financial crap, family shindigs, and other wonderful and delightful things are on your horizon.

But I'm here also to tell you that you can change direction. Yeah, you can CHANGE DIRECTION.

You don't have to head towards the cliff. You don't have to.

You can change direction. You can sooth your body, steep your soul with love, nourish your heart and stroke your mind.

All these things will shift you from the direction you are headed to, that cliff, to a whole other direction. The metaphor that comes to mind is of an oasis. Rather than heading to a cliff, head towards an oasis of love, of self care, of self preservation.

You can do it. I don't care how stubborn you are. How much you think that you are a lost case.

"Jonathan!" you may want to yell, "But you don't know me. This is WHO I AM! I've always been that way, since I remember myself!"

Oh yeah?

Then why do you waste my time and your time? There are plenty of other books with nice itty-bitty advises and things you can enjoy the thought of and never do.

You are here to be told the TRUTH.

The truth is that you can NEVER give someone from what you don't have. By you helping others and pleasing others and playing to other people's needs and expectations you are robbing yourself from the life that you deserve.

Let me repeat that. By pleasing others constantly, you are robbing yourself of the life that you deserve.

And yes, I'm talking about "others", being also

those precious hubby of yours, that wifie you adore, that child who still needs you, that friend who is in a real bad circumstances for the third time this year.

Oh, and I almost forgot: that parent that is really on your case and for no good reason.

You cannot give to them on your expense. Really. You are not helping them. Again: you are NOT helping them. You are making them collaborators in this robbery – in which you are both the robber and the victim.

Think of it, will ya?

"To love oneself is the beginning of a lifelong romance."

—Oscar Wilde
19th century Irish novelist

"Don't forget to love yourself."

Søren Kierkegaard

19th century Danish philosopher

LOVING YOURSELF

Will you allow me, for a moment, to speak to your SELF? To your inner voice? To the child inside you?

Hey there. I appreciate you being here. I appreciate the time you are taking to read this. I appreciate you.

Yes, I appreciate you.

In other words, I love you.

Yes, I know it may feel weird, to hear it, in such simple words.

But I really do.

I love you, you beautiful creation. I love all that you are.

Even the parts about you that you don't like. That you are afraid to show. I like these parts of you too.

I love each part of you.

I feel so sorry for all that you've been through. But now

it's time for you to relax into my embrace.

Hear my words, feel my warmth.

You are a child. All you seek for, in your multitude of ways, in your struggles to please – is love. You are seeking to be embraced, to be cared for. You want to be told how great you are.

And here I am, telling these words to you.

Will you listen?

Will you listen to me when I say that I'm sorry for hurting you?

I'm sorry for neglecting you.

I'm sorry for having abandoned you at times.

But now I'm here.

Yes, I know it will take time for you to fully trust me; for me to gain your full trust. But I'm not going anywhere.

There is freedom in my presence. There is everything you ever wanted – the joy, the care, the nourishment. It's here.

Will you listen when I tell you that I love you? That I really care for you?

I'm sorry at times I allowed myself to compare you, to judge you, to criticize you. I did that out of my own insecurities.

Not because I didn't love you.

I do love you.

I am here for you.

I am here to tell you that you are an angel. That your smile, your eyes, your voice – you are a true angel. You are so sweet that I don't think I'll be able to find the words to describe to you just how sweet you are.

And my love to you is so great, I'm unsure whether I'll be able to find the words to describe to you just how much I love you.

I love you. I really do.

It's simple. I don't ask you to do anything, or to prove yourself to me. From the moment you were conceived I loved you.

I will always love you.

I will love you when you don't feel worthy of my love. I nevertheless will love you.

I will love you when you judge yourself for not being successful enough yet. I will love you when you choose to compare yourself to others relentlessly. I will love you when you look in the mirror and are not overjoyed with the magnificence that you are.

I will sing for you, comfort you, hug and embrace you, direct you, guide you, nourish and feed you, I will clean you, wash you, heal your wounds, clothe you, take care of you in every way you desire.

The reason is, that I love you.

You were always deserving of this love. Yet you did not receive it. You therefore taught yourself that, actually, really, you do not deserve unconditional love. That as long as you work for it, and prove yourself, then and only then you are deserving of some love. Not much.

You have taught yourself a false teaching, my dear. It is false, I'm sorry.

As a baby, as a tiny baby, you were loveable. You were love. You were the epitome and the definition of what love is. You were so sweet, so good, so miraculous. You were.

Life has taught you wrongly. But I'm here now to correct this wrongdoing. The mere fact that you are reading these words shows that you resonate with them. That while you nevertheless may judge them as incorrect, somewhere inside you, you yearn for these words. The only reason for your yearning is that these words are true.

These are true words. It may take you time to fully comprehend them. You may resist, you may cry and protest. But the power of love will wash all over you, and calm your resistance.

This resistance that you developed was useful for you at one point. You developed it to survive. It helped you to cope, to stiff the upper lip and carry on. Had you demanded all that you deserved, you would have lived in a harsh reality of your needs being ignored and not fulfilled. Even laughed at.

So what you learnt to do is to minimize your needs. You looked at expression of love given to others, and you said, "I don't need that!" when in fact your heart yelped for that thing, for that thing exactly.

33

It's ok, we're just revealing the truth.

It may hurt, but it will feel much better.

The truth is that you deserved all the love that you didn't receive. And that there is nothing rude or unappreciative in saying that. You do recognize, at least when you are centered, that they have done everything they could and knew.

But now you realize that it wasn't enough. This realization does not blame or resent. It simply is.

What do you need this 'realization' for? Why do you need this painful acknowledgement from yourself to yourself that actually, no, you didn't receive all that you needed, all the love and all the caring.

This realization is important. This acknowledgement is crucial. Because it sets you free. It forces you to look to the truth in the eye, and accept it.

With this acceptance comes an inner sense of relief. Wow. I actually didn't get what I wanted. I actually deserved to get more. The thoughts that I asked for too much are actually judgments given to me by others. I adopted them, but now I can let them go.

Now I see that all that I craved for, I deserved to get. There was nothing snotty, rude, disrespectful, needy or spoiled in my needs to be loved unconditionally. There was nothing despiteful, spiteful, impolite or egoistic in me asking for what I wanted.

In fact, the contrary is true. When I indeed cried and fought for my birthright to be given love, attention, care, security – I was doing what a baby does when it cries, I notified and informed that I needed to be tended to, to be taken care of.

We can be so judgmental of that. Even the word "baby" has become affiliated with being 'needy', 'attention-grabbing' and 'immature'. Even the word "childish" has become a synonym for 'egoistic', 'rude' and 'impolite'.

But these words, "baby" and "childish" are of the most beautiful words ever created in the human language. Even in tribal times when words were just created, the word "baby" was one of the first to appear, and be told with love and care.

You asked for what you needed. You should not be ashamed, but proud. You did your share, you fulfilled the creation's purpose. A non demanding baby may very well be unable to communicate their most basic needs, and if that so, may actually not be able to survive.

I am stressing that to you, my baby, my child, so that you will walk proudly on this earth, saying, "I have asked for what I wanted. I did my share in the creation."

Then, at one point, you began seeing that when you asked for what you wanted, you did not always receive it. When you cried for love, you were sometimes assigned to be quiet in your room. When you struggled for attention you were reprimanded and hissed at.

And you learnt that you are undeserving of love.

Now you are unlearning that false learning. It is time.

"I didn't have a hard time making it, I had a hard time letting it go."

Elliott Smith

American singer-songwriter

"Accept yourself, love yourself."

Chanel Iman

American model and activist

BUT NOW YOU CAN GIVE YOURSELF

We need to realize that our resentment is eating us alive.

Now, even if you don't harbor difficult feelings towards your parents or caregivers, there is always some more to let go of.

At times it seems to me that, enough, I've already let it all go. I cried through it, I processed it, now it should be gone.

And then some times pass, and here something comes, and I'm like – not this one again!

I used to be upset by that.

But I realized over time that as we grow and develop, we'll encounter new layers, more profound, that we need to go through.

It's like a spiral. We've been here, it seems, but it's only the same area, not the same level.

So I wish to encourage you to let go.

What we are letting go of is resentment. We are letting go of the hope that things could have been different.

We let go of our disappointments and our pain.

And we choose to fill ourselves with the love we so craved from others.

Somewhere in time we were given the God-gift of creating our lives. We live the first part of our lives being a character in someone else's plot. We need them, we require them for our mere survival.

And then there comes a time in which we walk, we talk, we can feed ourselves, we can take care of ourselves.

And rather than feeling anger at those that didn't do a good enough job (and you may say, a lousy job in fact!), it's time for us to give love to ourselves.

Let's do it, God dammit.

"You have to choose
whether to love yourself
or not."

James Taylor

American singer and guitarist

"If you aren't good at loving yourself, you will have a difficult time loving anyone, since you'll resent the time and energy you give another person that you aren't even giving to yourself."

—Barbara de Angelis
American relationship consultant and author

MORE GOOD WORDS

I want to remind your subconscious few more things about yourself. So I'm going to speak as if I were you. Your brain will perceive these words written here as if they were your own. Feel free to read it slowly. Also, put some good music if you'd like. You can read it quietly or out loud. Whatever works for you. This comes with love from my heart.

Hey there. I'm so happy you are taking the time to read these lines.

Truth is, that I missed you.

It's been a while since I spoke to you. It's been a while since I spoke kindly to you.

I really care about you, you know?

Really.

Oh, I know I have a long way to go, 'till I'm able to

express my love to you better. I'm quite reticent when it comes to words of affection to you, you know? I'm sorry for that. I promise it's not going to be that always.

I promise you that there will be a time in which your inner chatter, in which I am the main voice, will be generally a kind one. I promise there will be a time in which I only share love with you. And when I do have advice or a critic, my words will be constructive and gentle.

Yep. I'm really sorry for having been so... harsh on you at times.

Do you hear me? I'm really really sorry for being harsh on you so often. You don't deserve that.

You deserve the best. You deserve kindness, care, gentleness. And I've failed you so many times.

Will you be willing to trust me again if I promised that I will be kinder to you? Oh please do. Please trust me.

You must also understand me. As your inner voice, I work day and night to help you. I try to save you from difficult situations, make sure you don't embarrass yourself, make sure you don't make yourself seem like an idiot – and more, making sure that people like you, that you are being needed and wanted by others, that people are impressed with you as much as I can make them... That has been my job, you see?

But I realize now this job has made you and I quite conflicted. I'm therefore willing to take a step back. I want to have a relationship with you, do you hear me?

I want us to be friends.

I want you and I, I and you, the whole YOU, made out of you and me, to be one. To be one again. Do you remember when we were young? I was rarely speaking to you. And quite frankly, I liked it better.

When I was just watching you being yourself, playing, making fun – that's when I had a much better time myself.

I hate being in war with you. I hate now that each time I tell you something you cringe. And I also hate that now, when I'm finally trying to tell you words of kindness – that you now don't believe me!

I hate that.

The reason I'm so flustered and… sad, really, is that I WANT a relationship with you. I really do.

Hey, please, I'm willing to change. I want us to be well together. I'm here to serve you. That was my original intention, when I began speaking up inside you, it was just to help you avoid the pain you felt. Remember the pain? Remember how unloved you felt? Well, this is why I began speaking to you, to protect you.

It's now that I realize that by constantly beating you down I actually suffocated you, and really… lost you.

I want to find you.

I want you to find me, ME, that voice you have inside, and for you to be pleased with what I tell you.

Because you do so much good, and you don't even see it.

Because you are wonderful, and you don't even know it.

Because you are really really beautiful, and you aren't even willing to entertain this thought!

I suffer seeing that you are not loving yourself.

And I hate thinking that me, your inner voice, had a huge part in it.

So, I'm changing. I am changing. With your encouragement, I can be the best inner voice ever. EVER! I can show you love, and kindness, and care, and tenderness – all those things that you deserve.

I can give you all that. And I want to. This is why I directed you to this book, to these words. Because I really care for you.

There is magic in this moment, of me speaking love to you. There is sacredness in me finally speaking softly to you. Do you hear me? Do you understand that I really do care about you?

I promise you that there will come a time in which these words won't feel foreign to you. There will come a time in which you feel my genuine love, your own genuine love to yourself. I promise you that.

I also promise you that one day, your cynicism and critic of these kinds of words, of these kinds of 'psycho babble' – your attitude will change. You are now just afraid, really. Behind all your cynicism there lies a fear. That I will tell you these words, that you will be willing to accept, and that I will then, out of the blue, batter you.

So, yes, what can I say. Your fear is justified. I have NOT been kind to you. Constantly critiquing and not loving. Far from loving.

But not only am I willing to change, I'm also changing right now, this very moment, in front of your eyes. I'm changing.

I tell you that no more will I treat you so badly. I will treat you well from now on. When you look in the mirror, you'll be able to see me, deep inside your eyes. When you close your eyes, you'll be able to feel me. When you go to sleep, I will caress you in your heart. I will protect you, nourish you, take a good care of you.

Because you are important to me.

You are. Important. To me.

Again, please do accept my apology. I'm here for you. FOR you. Not against you. I'm here to love you. And I will love you. I already do love you. I always loved you. Just didn't know how to express it, how to show it. Now I'm learning. Is it ok to learn? Is it ok for me to learn how to show you love in a way that will be good for you?

Please forgive me. I'm sorry. I forgive myself for my wrongdoings, as I know that they came out of real care and concern about you. I thank you for giving me another chance to be a loving voice within you. I love you, I really do.

"I am easy on myself. And I love myself like a newborn baby child."

—Karen Drucker
New Thought author and singer

"Every day brings a chance for you to draw in a breath, kick off your shoes, and dance."

—Oprah Winfrey
American media proprietor and philanthropist

YOUR GIFTS

I hope that last exercise was powerful for you. Thank you for cooperating with it, as much as currently feels comfortable for you. I recommend you reading it over and over, until you can muster the courage to write your own version. Then read it to yourself out loud. It sounds odd, but it's really powerful. I actually recorded it and I play it to myself over and over again. It's POWERFUL!

Now I want to talk to you about your gifts. You have so many unique gifts to give to the world. No one can do things the way you do.

If your current self esteem is low, you will resist these words. You will say, "well, how do you know?" and you will also think that I'm writing this for other people, not for you.

But I'm writing these words for each and every

human being reading. We all, ALL of us, have unique gifts. No two trees are similar. In fact, no two leaves are similar.

And no two people are similar.

You were born with a unique DNA that separates you from any other person. You were given talents, abilities and skills different than any other person.

When you resist loving yourself, when you refuse to have a healthy respect to yourself, when you decline to take good care of yourself – you rob the world of your gifts.

I'm going to use some harsh words, to make sure you get the message.

You, my love, are a thief. By trying to have everyone satisfied and gratified, by making sure everyone is appeased and pleased, you are robbing us all from your real self.

All the great creators in life, all the wonderful composers, actors, writers, statesmen, activists, artists – they all had one thing in common. It's one thing that you resist having. It's one thing that you would rather do without.

That thing is that they often put their wellbeing first. Yep. They did. Danielle Steel had to spend hours awake at night to write. It was important to her. It might have had an effect on her love life, or on her children. Yes, she tried to please everyone, but she also HAD to write. And write she did.

Oprah Winfrey again and again said things that

many people didn't want to hear. She fought to bring many gay people to her show, even though some viewers said, "enough with those gays!" But she stuck to it, to her truth. Part of why she is so loved is that she kept sticking to her truth, even if it wasn't popular.

While not necessarily well known today by many, Willy Brandt is considered one of Germany's best chancellors ever. Brandt took a pro soviet stance, at the pick of the cold war. He said that only through embracing the soviets can we avoid world war III. His dovish attitude, which included falling on his knees in front of a holocaust memorial in Poland, brought him many critics, who in fact almost succeeded to overthrow his government. But Brandt had felt the truth inside him, and was willing to compromise his popularity.

So did Lincoln, with the fight to end slavery. He received so many opponents for him voicing his opinions, and later on fighting for them. Martin Luther King Jr. too had to face much criticism. Many Christian leaders objected to his disobedience of the law, in what they saw as an un-Christian way. But King kept fighting for a cause he found just, even if others didn't approve of him.

I can go on and on in this list. It will show us that anyone who had ever accomplished anything worth while, did it while facing opposition.

Now, I hate opposition. And I would really like to have everyone like me. But I am coming to understand that that cannot be.

I recently posted some pro-peace stuff on my

Facebook page. While I did get few "likes" I actually got more negative comments. Most of my friends, who are Jewish and are traumatized by the Israeli-Arab conflict, think that by being pro-Arab, I must be also anti-Israel. And that's far from being the truth. I'm pro-everyone having the right to live in the beautiful Holy Land.

I tried to explain it, but I saw that some people wouldn't have my explanation.

The most difficult thing was to have family members critic my opinion, call me insane and naïve, and basically walk away from me.

Oh, it hurt.

It still hurts.

In an effort to calm myself I figured I should just freeze this post. Temporarily take it off. When I'm stronger, I thought, I will bring it back.

I looked at the options. No, not "Delete post". No, not "Hide from timeline". I want it frozen, gone for now.

I knew that if I hide it from the timeline, nevertheless people can still see it and comment. That basically all those who commented on it will be able to read the following comments, and continue to criticize me.

I was desperate. I wanted out. I told my wife I feel ambushed. By the same people who love me and give me many 'likes' whenever I post photos of our baby girl or of my art.

Having no other option, I chose "Hide from timeline."

To myself I thought, well, that doesn't show much confidence, hiding your opinions.

Yeah, well, ok, but neither is getting all this crap from others making me able to breath well.

But in the following day, and the day after, the Facebook comments kept coming. My aunt said, "Unfortunately Yoni you are living in supposed to be perfect world, however the reality is totally different and very grim, I think its time for you to face that reality and realize that very fast!"

My cousin said, "I'm appalled, just appalled by your insensitivity."

And I wanted to cry.

I told Hallel I cannot do it any more.

She advised me to delete the post and end with it.

As the mouse cursor hovered over the "Delete post" option, I sighed.

I believed in the words I wrote. I believed what I said was the right thing, that it's only through embracing and recognizing the other that we'll be able to live here in peace.

I thought that the fear and trauma that is leading all my friends and family to almost outcast me, is not the constructive way towards reconciliation. And I thought that ultimately, in their hearts, they want peace and reconciliation. They just don't know how to bring it to reality.

I felt that *I* knew. Having nearly 20 years of experience, hands on, in the peace scene, I've seen Arabs and Jews transform, open up, denounce violence. And the only thing that enabled them to do that was kindness, acceptance, embrace, listening to each other's stories and pain.

The mouse hovered over the "Delete post."

I can delete this post. Sure. One click and it will be behind me.

I can delete this post and shun my own opinions, even if I believe I'm right.

I can delete this post and let go of this temporary pain, this embarrassment, this feeling of becoming disliked by many people who until few days ago I was quite 'Liked' by.

I could.

But I then decided not to.

Life is too short to delete my opinions, erase my preferences, adjust my views according to others.

I didn't erase that post.

Rather, I let the thing slowly mellow down. After few days of the post being hidden from my Facebook timeline, those responding and corresponding began to seize.

And I felt more secure.

It's not that today I feel so much confidence as to write everything I think on my Facebook page. But, and this is a big BUT, I decide to stick to myself. I decide to love myself.

Loving yourself and putting yourself first is not popular. You will not get much signs of appreciation by those around you. Many will be surprised by you not being "nice" all of a sudden.

But the journey to loving yourself must go through putting yourself first. There is no other way.

Now, I'm not telling you to become aloof, to put yourself above others, to become anti-social. But I am telling you that you will NEVER be able to please EVERYONE.

And with that being said, why won't you choose to please yourself first?

Why won't you choose to please yourself FIRST?

Please entertain this question...? Why won't you put yourself first?

It's about time.

"Never explain yourself to anyone. You don't need anyone's approval. Live your life and do what makes you happy."

—Unknown

"When you stop chasing what your mind wants you will get what your soul needs."

—Unknown

LETTING GO

The first thing we must do to be ok with ourselves is love ourselves. Now, we've been exploring it now for quite a few pages. It sounds simple. But for most of us it's not.

I'm here to share with you my struggles in this journey, hoping the lessons I learnt through pain and struggle will help you.

The crucial thing to understand is that you are fighting a battle, that is the most important battle in your life.

There's a reason why I dedicate so much of this book to the need we all have to please others. This need, I believe, is the number one obstacle.

Because loving ourselves takes time. It takes practice. It's a habitual thing – something we'll add to our everyday routines. Some piece of time we'll schedule into every week. Treats and indulges we'll put into our life, as if our life depends on them.

And our life does depend on them.

You are being asked to put yourself first. You really are asked to do that.

The funny thing is that you have heard the opposite statement hundreds of times in your life.

Instead of hearing, "put yourself first" you heard, "be kind to him!"

"Be a lady!" (which means: don't show your real self)

"Be a man!" (which means: don't show your emotions)

"Be a grown up will ya?"

"Don't be a baby!"

"Now now, I want many things too but I don't get them!"

"Don't be selfish!"

"Don't be so needy!"

"Oh stop whining!"

"We'll get that for you later."

"You are way too noisy!"

Arrrrrghhhhh!

I bet you can add your own phrases to this list.

Now, I'm not blaming our parents and the grown ups around us. They did the best they can. But it's no shame to say that their best wasn't enough.

Let's have a look for a second at those figures who spoke that way and modeled this unhealthy and wrong outlook – that you need to put other people's needs first.

For example, I had a grandmother who used to not complain at all. She died from cancer in her sixties.

I was five, barely knew her.

My father says, "Oh, I wish she would have complained more, not held everything inside…"

Not that my father is such a great example of the opposite. Remember, we model what we see.

My father also sticks to phrases that can be detrimental.

For example, he says, "family must come first."

Now, I agree. But not to the extent that family comes BEFORE yourself.

We kids constantly tell him to learn how to say "no", to us, to our mother, to relatives. Since he doesn't know how to do that, he runs around doing errands and he is constantly exhausted. Recently he complained to me that he wants to go on a vacation already. When he and my mother go to a vacation far away, no one can expect him to do anything, and he then feels free, stronger, better, healthier.

I told him what I'm telling you. You need to change some of your beliefs, and learn to put yourself first. What's good in going to a vacation if three days after you come back you're already swamped with to-dos for everyone but yourself?

I'm all for vacations, believe me, I LOVE vacations. But my dad, me, and you, need to all learn how to embed the qualities of a proper vacation in our day to day life.

My father especially likes going abroad. There's a reason for that. There, his cellphone doesn't work. It works on Wi-Fi, and he can receive Facebook and Whatsapp messages. Sometime he also buys a local SIM card wherever they are. But the main thing is that his phone doesn't ring.

When in the country, my dad's cellphone rings constantly. Old aunts and an assortment of I-need-help-now friends call him. Since he had not mustered the art of saying 'no' he has come to long for vacations. Far away vacations, abroad.

He never-ever turns his cellphone off. He wants to always be available in case something happens. But this doesn't help his relationship with my mom, and I think more importantly, it doesn't help the relationship he has with himself.

Ariana Huffington of the Huffington Post recently shared how at night she sets a nice and relaxed atmosphere in her bedroom, sometimes lighting candles, etc. She doesn't allow her cellphone to enter the bedroom.

Let me repeat: she doesn't allow her cellphone to enter the bedroom. She says that if she finds that her cellphone had somehow infiltrated the sacred space of the bedroom she "gently escort him out of the room."

I like that.

That feels to me like she is getting it.

We have to set clear boundaries. If we don't everyone will have a piece of us.

Will you set a clear boundary? It's a must if you want to begin practicing habits of self love, that in turn will change your inner dialogue to a more loving one. The benefits are huge: happiness, joy, authenticity, a feel of ease. But you need to start from setting clear, very clear boundaries.

"Lend yourself to others,
but give yourself to
yourself."

—Michel de Montaigne
14th century French philosopher

"When you give yourself, you receive more than you give."

— Antoine de Saint-Exupery
French writer and poet

PRIORITIZING YOURSELF

When you prioritize yourself first, you have enough time to feel good, to feel replenished. You fill your cup fully. Then, when your cup is full, you can give others from the overflow.

Never ever give others from what you don't have.

This means that saying 'no' must become comfortable for you.

It wasn't for me.

I used to say 'yes' for everything, modeling after both my father and my mother. It was not good for me. In my mid twenties I had several charities I was volunteering for, being on the boards of directors, while doing all kinds of other stuff too.

It was fulfilling. But simultaneously it was draining. How could that be?

Well, whenever someone would give me a good word, show me that they appreciate me, I'd feel much better. Also, when I saw that someone, a student of mine (I taught the language Esperanto to new students), a mentee of mine (I volunteered as Big Brother for a kid), or the organization as a whole made a progress – that progress would fill me and make me pleased.

But what when there was no appreciation from others, or when no progress was to be seen? Then I'd feel drained, exhausted, unappreciated, and tired, really really tired.

At the time I was taking a part in a "mastermind group", which basically meant a group of individuals that were into personal growth. The six of us would meet on Skype every other week, would share some of our challenges, and offer advice and encouragement to one another. It was quite powerful, because I took many lessons from it.

One of the lessons I took was an exercise. I think I lamented out loud the fact that I'm sooooo busy and exhausted. When I was asked why, I gave a partial (very partial) list of all the things I was involved with.

It was then that one of the participants in the mastermind group said to me she'd like me to try an exercise for the following two weeks.

"What is it?" I asked, not wanting to add yet another chore to my list.

"Once a day say 'no' to something."

"Say 'no?'"

"Yeah," she said, "it sounds simple, but it's

powerful."

"No," I said, "it doesn't sound simple at all."

But I liked that idea. So I decided to give it a shot.

Three days later I was still not practicing this exercise. There was no opportunity to say no, I felt.

But I kept thinking about it. Also, I received an email from the mastermind, listing each person's commitment till our next meeting.

I was already behind on my commitment.

"We need volunteers," the email read, "among you Big Brothers, to help setting up the picnic next Friday."

I looked at it, and triumphantly pressed the Reply. "Hi Rickie, I'm excited about the picnic, but unfortunately won't be able to help."

Before sending I added, "but if you need anything done that actual same day, please tell me."

I then deleted this added sentence.

And then I wrote it back. "If you need anything on that actual Friday, let me know."

And then I deleted it. Fuck, learn how to say 'no'!

Then I hit "Send" and jumped off my seat – "I did it!"

And this was just the beginning.

"But I always had the ability to say no. That's how I called my own shots."

—Sidney Poitier
Bahamian-American actor and author

"Learn to say 'no' to the good so you can say 'yes' to the best."

—John C. Maxwell
American author and pastor

SEEKING YOUR OWN APPROVAL

You got to be worried more about how YOU will FEEL than about what OTHERS will THINK.

When I wrote that email to Rickie saying I won't be able to help, I immediately thought "how will she respond? What will she think of me?"

But over the years, the more I learnt to say no since then, the more I realized it's not important what she will think. I'm not responsible for her thoughts.

In fact, if she's smart, Rickie may think, "Wow, good for him, he knows how to say no."

Or she may think, "Great, Jonathan knows how to set his boundaries. That's a good modeling for his young brother he's mentoring."

Or she may think, "Jonathan – wow, I should learn from him. He said 'no' but did it in such a fine manner."

Whatever she thinks, it's none of my business.

These days I got into a really healthy discipline: I don't say 'no' and I don't say 'yes'. I say, "Can I get back to you tomorrow on that?"

"But Jonathan," I may hear the person asking for the help saying back, "I need to know now, and I can't imagine who I'll have to ask if YOU won't be able to help me!"

"Yeah, I totally understand," I answer, "but I'm sorry, I have to look into what I've already committed to, and see, I don't want to promise you and then disappoint you, you see? So let me get back to you on that tomorrow."

This already seeds the seed of the OPTION that I may say no.

In the following 24 hours, the person who asked me has to come up with some alternate solutions, in case I will say no.

Then, when I do say no, or when I do offer to do just a small part in my proposed chore, the person on the other side doesn't take it as bad.

Try it, it works wonders. Next time a person asks you to help with something, even if you're SURE you'll say yes, tell them you'll get back to them on that tomorrow.

It makes people respect you more. And guess who else it makes more respectful of you?

"What other people think of you is none of your business."

—Paulo Coelho
Brazilian novelist and lyricist

"As a parent, if give yourself what you need, your children will watch you doing that and will give themselves what they need."

—Susan Cain
American writer and lecturer

THE TRUTH

If you are afraid about saying 'no' to others more often, and the consequences it may bring, let me NOT reassure you.

In fact, let me make you worried. Because we need to look into that.

When you begin to shine, some people won't like it. When you follow your own desires, some people will be upset. We spoke about that.

Some people will actually leave. Yep. They will actually find you unhelpful.

And that's ok.

This might cause a little bit of reorganizing of your personal and social life. You want people around you who are supportive of you because of who you ARE rather than because of what you DO.

And if they leave, you might get into a panic attack. You might be afraid of you not having friends. And you might be afraid of not having the old gratification that you used to receive.

But ultimately, over time, this will do you a great service.

You can't grow to fully love yourself and embrace yourself when you are constantly trying to meet other people's demands, and when you are being measured by other people's expectations.

With time you will find that the shift you had in your life was one of the best things that happened to you.

Not that it's going to be easy.

You might go through a time of a separation anxiety. You might want to run back and say, "OK, OK, I'll put myself second, but please come back!"

The reason I'm saying this is that I personally found myself in this situation more than once. And now I am feeling much lighter, of people, even very close to me, who expected me to act in one very certain way, and when I didn't, they simply left in a storm.

I have one relationship with a close friend, we were like brothers. But he constantly was assisted by me. Not only technical things, but also emotionally. He dominated most of the conversations, and was quite negative. He also expected of me to always be there, while when I was asking for him to be there for me, he was quite busy, and I needed "to understand."

Now, I'm not blaming him. I was the one to follow his direction, and not put any boundary. I basically fulfilled his dream of a best friend, while he didn't fulfill mine, nor were he any close.

But I put him on a pedestal, and, well, when someone is on a pedestal, it may cause you to break your neck.

When it became too much for me, and my emotional 'neck' was breaking, I tried to speak with him. He asked me to do a favor. And I felt like he was asking it in a too matter-of-fact manner, not really ASKING, but almost REQUESTING.

So I tried to say, "Well, I'd like to help, but I must say that recently I've been feeling like I do for you, and that you don't really... appreciate it."

Unfortunately he wouldn't have it.

"Let me not go into everything I've done for you," he said, "and we're friends, I'm just asking for you to help me in this little thing!"

"Yeah," I said, "but last time I helped you didn't even say thank you, or acknowledged the time I had put into it. You actually showed your dissatisfaction with HOW I did it. And it was a FAVOR I was doing for you."

He expected me to be a certain way. And based on many years or our relationship, and on help he had given me early on, he thought that I had MUCH to do and was far from having the luxury of expressing my dissatisfaction.

And so, after I told him I felt that he didn't appreciate all that I was doing, he basically said, "Man, this is too much for me to hear right now, and I'm also in a really busy time these days."

"But," I said, "I want us to speak about it, and see, and for each of us to express what he feels, and hopefully—"

"Well, I can't right now, so, I just CAN'T, right now."

He hasn't called since.

I texted him, and he said he was swamped and 'taken aback' by what I said, and that it's going to take him some time.

"I'm here." I wrote back.

And haven't heard from him since.

Was I too offensive?

Was I wrong to expect him to listen?

Should I have helped again, at least this one time?

"No way!" Hallel told me. "You've been complaining about this relationship since I know you, for four years. Give him the time. You did what you had to do."

"But," I struggled, "what if he won't...?"

"Then he won't," Hallel said, "and you would know that you SPOKE and said how you FELT, and that he wasn't willing to listen."

It still hurts me to write that.

And I still hope he will call and we could make the relationship work. We were good friends. I believe we can make it work, if I would know to put my boundaries.

So what I'm trying to say here is that yes, sometimes it might cause a havoc when you are standing for your self. If you insist on putting yourself first and giving yourself first, some will find it troubling.

But it's OK.

It's OK.

"If there is someone in your life who is not serving you or making you better, give yourself permission to move on."

— Niecy Nash
American comedian and producer

"Dedicate yourself to the good you deserve and desire for yourself. Give yourself peace of mind. You deserve to be happy. You deserve delight."

—Hannah Arendt
Holocaust survivor and political theorist

YOU ARE THE ANSWER

And so YOU are the answer for your question. You are the cause of your suffering and your pain. You can choose to think differently and act differently, and then rip the fruits.

You can start by making a list, each time completing the following sentence:

If I truly loved myself, I would…

I would, for example, walk in nature more.

I would smile to myself more in the mirror.

I would buy myself some new clothes and get read of some old ones.

I would publish more things on Facebook.

I would tell myself that my books and paintings are GREAT.

I would wash away thoughts about what I "should" have done in certain circumstances.

I would eat better.

I would say 'no' more often (still working on it!)

I would play the guitar more.

I would dance more.

I would sit at the end of the workday and write my accomplishments, rather than focus on what I haven't finished yet.

I would take a nice long bath with candles and relaxing music.

Do you see what I'm saying here? YOU must be the solution. YOU must give to yourself.

The world will then notice that you treat yourself better. That you walk in a certain way, talk in a certain way, carry yourself in a certain way – that you love yourself.

And the world will follow suit.

I promise.

Now take a moment to think for yourself:

If I truly loved myself, I would...

"Sometimes you just got to give yourself what you wish someone else would give you."

—Dr. Phil McGraw
American psychologist and TV personality

"The greatest gift that you can give yourself is a little bit of your own attention."

—Anthony J. D'Angelo
American author and speaker

SELF-LOVE VS. CONCEIT

One of the questions I hear all the time is "isn't being all that loving towards yourself a bit... conceited?"

If I then ask and inquire, these are the typical phrases I hear: "Well, I just don't want to come out as too full of myself, you know?" Or "I hate people that are boastful and conceited, so I don't want to be like them."

Alright. Let's make things clear, as you may be thinking these same thoughts.

Self-love is the furthest thing from conceit, or having excessive pride in oneself. Self-love is not necessarily anything others will notice from the outside. If anything, they will notice that you FEEL better and are DOING better, or that you RADIATE love and kindness. They will not, and I repeat, they will NOT think that you are being arrogant if you are treating yourself well.

On the contrary. I think that arrogance and conceit are a result of not loving yourself ENOUGH. When you really love yourself, you don't feel the need to prove yourself or to boast of your successes, because you feel really good and satisfied. You feel loved, and you are not starving for other people's approval.

When someone isn't loving themselves enough, they will long for all kinds of external validation, such as being called by their credentials, receiving the credit for other people's work, having others listen to them excessively, etc. These are not signs of self love, but of a deprivation of self love.

Basically, by judging them and saying, "boy, is he arrogant or what" or "she's so full of herself and of big-headed" you are quick to make a common mistake.

We all make this mistake.

We judge the external behavior and assume that it means that the person is an admirer of themselves.

But the truth is that often, well actually let me say ALWAYS, the case is the reverse. If they truly and wholly loved themselves, they would have insisted on sharing love with others, from their overflow.

As they don't have enough love, and do not know of how to give it to themselves, they seek it from others.

So be loving and accepting of such behavior, as long as it does not take from your own wellbeing. Send these people love in your thoughts – they are just abandoned children seeking for validation and approval, like we all do. Their case is just a sadder one.

Your fear of being labeled as aloof or a snub due to loving yourself must be called off here. As a result of loving yourself you will only be able to love others, be more patient and kind to others, and in turn, be more loved by others.

And besides, we've been through it. Even if you practice self-love and self-care, and some people don't like it, it's non of your business. You have to set a model for them, and for all of us, as to how to treat ourselves.

Please give us a good model, OK?

"Sometimes it's okay to give yourself a pat on the back and say, 'That was cool. That made me feel good.'"

—Sebastian Stan
Romanian-American actor

"There's nothing wrong with giving yourself a pat on the back. If you can't do that, you can't be objective about your work. You can't be conceited or cocky, but you can't be too modest either."

—Jack Reynor
Irish actor

I WILL LOVE MYSELF WHEN…

One common mistake we all fall to is the notion that "I will love myself, WHEN I will finish my degree" or "I will give myself love when I get this promotion" or "When my children appreciate me, that's when I will be at ease."

Bad bad baaaad. This is not good at all – yet we all do that.

Why can't we decide that TODAY we'll be appreciative of ourselves? Why can't we begin to count our many accomplishments this very day? Why do we wait?

Again, I think this is something we need to be TAUGHT. And as our parents didn't know how to do it themselves, we simply copied them.

But now we know better.

Now we are older and wiser.

It's time for us now to take a conscious decision to really love who we are.

There's nothing bad in doing that.

There's no 'self-love-police' that will come and chase us down and put us in jail.

This reminds me of how once, when I was about six years old or so, I began taking few coins from my dad's pants, hanging in the bathroom at night.

Those coins, boy, were they useful! They got me some nice treats in the grocery store, I was in HEAVEN.

Then my mom opened my pencil box one day, and found those coins.

"Who gave these to you?" she asked with a severe look.

"I... no one!" I said and tried to walk away.

My mom then grabbed my arm and raised her voice. "Where did you get these coins?"

My poor mom. As an adult I realize she was probably afraid someone was giving the coins to me in return for some unhealthy conduct. Or something like that. She was really worried.

"I..." I finally whispered, as I knew what I did was wrong, "I got them out of dad's pants, hanging on the bathroom door..."

By then my mom was flustered and emotional, and she said, "Why did you take it? Are you a thief? Do you want me to call the police and have them take you to children's prison? Do I need to call the police?"

"No…" I said, about to cry.

"Then promise me you won't take any coins without permission!"

"I promise!" I muttered and thought, please, just let me go!

She then left me alone.

I felt really bad.

And for years later I was afraid of that children's police that was to come and take me to children's prison.

Few years ago I spoke about it with my mom. She did not remember. She apologized. I explained she could have spoken more softly. We later hugged.

But I think that as grown ups, we still walk with our parents' reprimand in our head.

Well, let me tell it to you now. No police will come and take you if you acknowledge yourself and love yourself.

Nothing good is going to come out of you always striving to be your best on the expense of your own wellbeing.

Please, let go of the unreal expectations you have set for yourself. The road of self-battering is not a good one for you. Today you can leave that road and take the path of self-love, self-respect, self-nurturing.

The only question is, will you?

"If your mother did not know how to love herself, or your father did not know how to love himself, then it would be impossible for them to teach you to love yourself."

—Louise L. Hay
American motivational author and healer

"To love yourself right now, just as you are, is to give yourself heaven. Don't wait until you die. If you wait, you die now. If you love, you live now."

—Alan Cohen
American author and columnist

STOP WITH THE CRICITISM

What if today was your last day here on earth? Would you still treat yourself the way you treat yourself right now?

Most people's answer to that question is "nope." If indeed this was your last day, you would most likely express more love. Not only to others, but also to yourself.

If this is your last day, you'd probably throw away your "I'm always such a loser" or "here you are late again!" or "I should have seen it coming, what an awful mom I am!"

You would have been EASIER on yourself. You would have allowed yourself to be a little more content with yourself.

The only purpose of your self-reprimand, if there is any purpose, is for you to change in the future as a result of your reprimand.

But what if... you didn't have any future? What if this day WAS indeed your last day. Surely, one day it WILL be your last day. So why are you criticizing yourself so much?

Let it go. Let harsh words go. Let expressions of exasperation with yourself become something of old. Let all your explanations of why you are not as good or successful as you would have liked become old leaves that have fallen from the tree. Let it go.

Even as I'm writing this book, the voice of self-criticism comes to me often. It says, "who the heck is going to read this book anyhow?" and "it's a bunch of bull you put together and dare calling it a book?" and "it will be quite transparent to your readers that you don't know what you're talking about!"

Yep. My inner voice still can go off in a tandem sometimes. It's still not where I'd like it to be.

But it's definitely WAY better than it used to be.

I can quietly tell it, "Thank you so much for your advice, but really, love, no need. I'm OK."

And instead of fighting back, like it always did, these days it says, "Oh, OK then, tell me if you need me."

Also, as a way to practice what I've been preaching, if you indeed think that I don't know what I'm writing about, or that this book is a bunch of bull, then, thank you – but what you think about me or this book is NONE of my business. I LOVE it. And I LOVE MYSELF. Godammit! I do. I struggled to get here, and I pat myself on the back, kiss myself on the front, and embrace myself on the inside.

Ha ha!

"Give yourself permission to toot your own horn, and don't wait for anyone to praise you."

—Jack Canfield
American motivational author and speaker

"Don't ever criticize yourself. Don't go around all day long thinking, 'I'm unattractive, I'm slow, I'm not as smart as my brother.' God wasn't having a bad day when he made you!"

—Joel Osteen
American preacher and author

BECOMING A STAR

I recently watched an interview in which Oprah Winfrey interviewed First Lady Michelle Obama. At one point during the interview Oprah commented, "yes, I believe in service, I believe in helping people, I want people to feel fulfilled and empowered in their life," and then added, "but still some days I think, it's just cool to be me."

The audience then laughed and cheered. Oprah's words may sound like she was a little full of herself. But her words came to serve as inspiration for all of us. We all need to treat ourselves as if we were stars, as if it was "really cool to be us."

You may say, "If I were Oprah, I would think it's cool to be me!"

But I think we all have things to be grateful for, and reasons to think we are quite cool. Here, let's do a quick exercise: What makes you "cool?"

My turn: Well, I'm cool because I am a really fun dad, and I do all kinds of fun stuff with my baby girl Sarah.

Your turn:

My turn: I'm super cool because I dance pretty well and I feel pretty free.

Your turn:

My turn: I'm cool cause I have a really fine smile. Really. I have a great smile.

Your turn:

My turn: I'm cool because I dare to be vulnerable and express my emotions.

Your turn:

My turn: I'm cool because I'm just cool. I am cool, the epitome of cool, I'm what you'll find in the dictionary under Coolness, I'm cool cool cool real cool cool indeed. Yeah!

Your turn: (let's see you after that!)

My turn: I'm cool because I lead my life. When it was time for us to move to the north I found the proper house for us to rent and signed the lease, even though Hallel wasn't sure. Now she thanks me for acting fast, and she loves the house. That's pretty cool – acting and daring to take brave decisions.

Your turn:

My turn: Well, we can go on for a while, right? Here's my last cool reason. I'm cool because I AM. I'm cool because I was BORN. I'm cool because I have this body to explore this planet with. I'm cool because I'm the outcome of this one daring sperm to hit this egg and make ME. I'm cool because I don't NEED to find any reason why I'm cool. I'm cool because I AM.

Your turn:

Now that we finished, why won't you go back and actually do this exercise? ;)

"You're not a star until you love yourself. Directors, yeah, they've got to love their own philosophies. But actors have to really love themselves."

—Shekhar Kapur
Indian film director, actor and producer

"If you don't love yourself, you can't love anybody else. And I think as women we really forget that."

—Jennifer Lopez
American singer and actress

"BUT YOU DON'T KNOW MY STORY!"

One of the thoughts you have on your mind may be, "Well, that's very nice for YOU, Jonathan, but you don't know MY story."

That's true. But quite frankly, if your story is what keeps you from blossoming to be your WHOLE self, then I wouldn't want to hear it.

We all have stories. True, some people's stories are more difficult than others. Many people have to go through various forms of abuse, which definitely lowers one's self esteem to the floor. It's really a HUGE challenge to overcome having experienced abuse of any sorts.

But I have come to believe that everything we've been through was an intentional thing. That it all was part of a plan to make us who we are.

My father hit me few times. I wouldn't call it abuse,

but it definitely wasn't something I like to remember, or that I intend to pass on to my own kids.

For years I held it against him. And I was afraid of him to an extent.

Nowadays I see it, though, as one of the most important things that shaped me to be who I am. I am one of the most sensitive guys you'd meet – I feel people's pain, I can easily relate, and I allow myself to experience and hurt WITH them.

I think part of this gift was actually the negative experience of having my father go after me and slapping me in my bottom. It was painful, burningly painful. And humiliating too.

But today I think it made me part of who I am.

When I was young my mom would often burst out in shouting and yelling, often being quite unkind in her punishments. What was so unique was that I couldn't expect it. She was altogether a really loving mom, warm and nourishing. And yet, at times, she could be really mad and unreasonable, to the extent I couldn't converse with her, but had to just be silent.

This experience of my mom possibly having the possibility of having a sudden fit, made me become extra aware. I tried to see in her movement and her face whether she was tired or bothered, which were the indications that something may erupt.

I learnt to watch her move, watch her facial expressions, her eyebrows, her forehead, even the slightest move of her lips: were they tight? Tight-ish? Tense? And how about her shoulders? And her breath?

I learnt to be extra sensitive, and I knew to walk away fast when she was going to have a fit. And all of that when I was five years old or so.

Years later, I was at the seventh grade, and took part in the school's student council. We were students from the seventh grade all the way up to the twelfth grade. Once we were given a lecture by a teacher who specialized in body language.

She showed us different body postures with a overhead projector. There were many. She then asked us, each time, what did we think: was this person (a) upset (b) worried (c) scared, or (d) surprised.

Some of the slides were easy, some were more complicated. She showed us some twenty of them, including ones of couples (were they resentful or loving? Worried or hopeful?).

Each of us wrote the answers down after each slide, and at the end the teacher told us the right answer, and asked us to mark a check mark if we got the correct answer. "Now count how many you got right."

I counted. She then asked, "how many of you had ten correct answers or less?" No one raised their hand. "How about eleven?"

Two students raised their hands. "Good job!" the teacher said. "And twelve?"

Few more raised their hands. The same was with 13 correct answers. Then for 14 there was only two people.

"Anyone got above 14 correct answers?" the teacher asked.

I looked at my sheet, alarmed. It said "18".

I said nothing. Yet Rinat, a 12th grader who was the head of the student council, sat next to me and glanced at my paper. "Common," she whispered.

But I didn't want to say anything.

"Jonathan has!" Rinat said triumphantly, "he has 18 correct answers!"

The teacher looked flustered, and came and hovered above my sheet. "Wow," she said with a smile, "that's impressive. Now let's go over each one and try to see what were the physical indications of each state."

Even today, remembering this lecture, I blush.

We looked at each slide, and she asked what made us think the person was happy or sad. There were the obvious things which everyone recognized, and then there were more subtle things. The teacher was impressed with my soft-spoken comments.

I believe it was due to having somewhat of a turbulent childhood. I developed skills that I link and attribute to the unfortunate circumstances of my mother throwing incidental fits.

Now, would I have preferred that those fits didn't happen? Probably. Am I upset by them? Not so much, not anymore.

Each and every experience you had brought you to this moment. Each and every difficult moment made you who you are now. Embrace your whole self. Embrace all of your experiences, good and bad.

Yes, you are right. I DON'T know your story. But author Lisa Nichols says: "Your mess is your message." Make your 'Story', that thing that holds you back, the foundation on which you climb to become taller.

It's up to you. Maya Angelou did it, Oprah Winfrey did it, and YOU can do it too. Rewrite your story. Actually sit and WRITE it. Find out ALL the advantages, big and small, that came from the fact they left you. Write down everything you learned from being estranged from your child. Write down why your first spouse was valuable to you nevertheless. Write down why that cousin actually did you a service.

I know it hurts. But you OWE it to yourself. Rewrite your story.

"Whatever trauma you've had, you can still love yourself."

—Patch Adams
American physician, clown, and social activist

"It's one of the greatest gifts you can give yourself, to forgive. Forgive everybody."

—Maya Angelou
American poet, author, and activist

LETTING GO OF RESENTMENT

One of the greatest obstacles to us loving ourselves like we should is resentment.

We think that if we let go of the anger and blame, we become "collaborators" with the perpetrator.

Let's have a look at that.

In the ninth grade I joined Israel's most prestigious art school. There I majored in theatre. It was quite an extensive program, one similar to that portrayed in the movie "Fame." We had dance lessons, voice lessons, costume lessons, make up and masks lessons, and, of course, acting lessons.

The acting teacher we were given was Jacob. He was considered one of Israel's greatest acting and drama teachers. The other teachers told us this fact several times. He was the founder of the street theatre and performance movement in Israel. He studied in France with the famed Jacques Lecoq, and was quite well known himself in Israel.

The only problem was that he didn't like me. At all.

Jacob had strong opinions. He was a very charismatic man, then in his late sixties. He had fiery eyes. And when he said something, you believed him.

For some reason, I wasn't his cup of tea. While most students got their crams of compliments, no leftover crams were handed to me. He thought I was too this and too that. He thought I was too sensitive. Not much of a young man for him.

He marveled at some of the more manly looking boys in class, and said, "I can sit and watch you and melt from your fire," and then he'd look at us, "can't you?"

And we would all nod. Yeah, he's right. Fire, right.

Oh, how I longed to be said I had any sort of fire. I worked and labored hard. Each assignment, such as watching a cat walk and later being able to mimic it exactly – I would go down to the street and look for cats, watch their every movement. Then practice in my room.

"Not that way, Jonathan!" Jacob would exclaim exasperated. We had white masks on, with only the eyes showing. I looked at him, this was supposed to be a silent exercise, and we only now began, why does he pick me to critic? I tried to say, "But I studied it!" but my voice sounded thick through the mask with no opening for the mouth.

"Now, listen to me," he commanded, "right hand forward, then left knee forward, now left hand forward, now right knee forward... that's right."

That's exactly what I did. Why did he have to...? Why?

Once I stood on stage, alone, him watching me with the rest of the class. Then he said, "but you have no presence, no command of the stage..." and he put his hand on his forehead in exasperation.

What was so frustrating is that all the other kids adored him. Even the students from the higher grades. They said, "he may be tough, but wait till next year, everything will fall into place."

Shifra, my favorite teacher, said, "Jacob is a genius. You students should feel honored to be studying with him." Everyone nodded.

I tried to approach him once before class. When he saw my face he looked tired. "Yes, Jonathan?"

"I..." I said, "I want to know what should I do to be... better, to be a better actor."

Jacob sighed a long sigh. He looked at me. "The thing is, boy, that you don't have any presence. You are transparent on stage, I can see through you."

I already heard that. "But what can I do?"

"Eat bread, lots of bread."

"Bread?"

"Yes, bread. Now, let's go into class."

I walked after him, bewildered. Bread?

Yet no matter how much bread I ate, his attitude to me didn't change.

At the end of the year he said, "Students, I have an announcement to make. I will not be continuing with you next year."

Everyone gasped. Me too. I was looking forward to seeing how he could 'put it all together' like I was told so many times – 'Jacob will tare you apart, to then saw you back together as a whole actor in your second year, it will all fall into place.'

We looked at him with amazement. "But why?" some of us asked.

"Well, many reasons," he said, "but you will be fine. They will bring you a good teacher, one that will keep where we stopped."

To myself I was thinking, 'but I'm torn open. You promised to complete this…'

The next year teacher didn't know Jacob's hierarchy of who was a brilliant actor and who wasn't. Somehow, by grace from above, he liked me. Slowly, my self esteem began healing.

Few years ago I met with a friend from school, whom I haven't seen for a decade or so. We had coffee in a café in north Tel Aviv. And we spoke among other things about school.

I was surprised to hear that she had lots of criticism at the school. "Teachers exercising their authority in a wrong way," she said.

I wondered what she meant. For me, the story and the emotions attached to that Jacob teacher were stuffed into a compartment in my heart I was only tiptoeing around, afraid to awaken any old hurts.

"Well, do you remember how Albert, the choreography teacher used to light his cigarette in class?" she asked.

Oh yes. "Yeah, that was quite stupid."

"Or how the musical director told us we are 'a bunch of useless armatures' and that we should 'fuck off'?"

"Oh my god."

"And don't get me started about Jacob."

I looked at her. Actually, I thought, I'd like for you to get started about Jacob. Back in the day I could confide my pain in no one. And I hadn't really opened it or touched it since then.

"What do you remember of Jacob?" I asked.

"He was just so…" she was looking for the right word, "cruel."

"Cruel?" I asked. Was she not using a too harsh of a word?

"What?" she looked at me, surprised, "don't you remember how he talked to you, of all people?"

"I do…" I said. It felt so good to know that she noticed. "It's… nice to see that you took note."

"Took note?! It was as visible as it could be. Do you remember that comment he made about your… 'sausage'?"

I couldn't not laugh. "Sausage? Nope…"

"Wow," she stared at me, "I can't believe you don't remember it. You were standing on stage, in front of all of us, and he asked you," Michelle lowered her voice, 'Do you have a sausage down there or a hot dog bun?'"

Wow. I remembered it. All of a sudden it came to me.

Jacob was not stupid. At the time I wasn't quite sure myself.

I looked at Michelle. "I remember."

"Do you remember how it continued?"

I thought for a moment. "No…"

Michelle sighed. Everyone became quite, and he asked you again, 'Do you have a sausage or a bun?'

"You said, 'a sausage', and he said, 'good.' And then he said, 'now, is your sausage interested in buns, or in other sausages?'

I looked at Michelle, "Oh my god. I can't believe he said that."

"Neither do I," Michelle said.

We both sat there in silence. I tried to remember, what did I answer? Probably that I was interested in buns, of course.

Thinking of it made me feel a little sick to my stomach, and then a wave of sadness washed over me.

I sighed.

I remembered how some three years before, at the

age of 25, I went to a meditation retreat. In it, the teacher asked us to forgive everyone who had ever hurt us.

I asked myself then, 'who should I forgive?' and then Jacob's face came before me.

I said, 'I forgive you.'

But then, in front of Michelle in that Tel Aviv café, I felt so much anger at this stupid old man, terrorizing me in front of the whole class.

Which answer should I have given him? 'I don't know'? 'Well, I'm still struggling with this question myself?' or 'Well, my last girlfriend told me I must be gay, because I told her of this wet dream I had about me and an imaginary guy, so…?'

Michelle looked at me. "He was exercising his power over you in a way that was not OK."

"Yeah," I said.

Now, it's time to forgive. Really forgive. Follow me.

"I think the first step is to understand that forgiveness does not exonerate the perpetrator. Forgiveness liberates the victim. It's a gift you give yourself."

—T. D. Jakes
American pastor, author and filmmaker

"The weak can never forgive. Forgiveness is the attribute of the strong."

—Mahatma Gandhi
Indian leader, philosopher and activist

FORGIVENESS EXERCISE

Let's continue from where we stopped in the last chapter. I hope this inner dialogue I have with myself will serve as an example for you as to how to truly forgive.

So, Jacob. I resent the fact that you abused the power and the authority you had over me as a teacher. I resent the fact you treated me badly, marked me as a student to pester and to taunt.

I resent the fact that you called me names, and treated me disrespectfully. I resent that you did all that. That you abused, really abused your position as a teacher. A teacher is supposed to nurture, guide, direct, and you did NOT do that. You messed up. You failed in your task as a teacher.

Whatever philosophy you supposedly had behind your dumb actions and statements, I find it faulty. Students should not be put down in order to 'lift them up' later. It's dumb, I strongly and adamantly disagree with this method. It's wrong. Wrong.

And not only did you abused your power, you did it in front of the whole class. You humiliated me and terrorized me, really, in front of the whole class. That was not fair. If you had any constructive critic you could have given it to me in private.

I resent the fact you smiled when the students chuckled. I resent that it gave you a sense of power and authority, to humiliate one of your students, less than half your age – less than a quarter of your freakin' age!

I am angry with your misguidance, with your snobbery, with how you implied all the time that you had all the answers, and that we were just in our beginning stage. You did not empower me. You disempowered me, and I allowed you to do that.

Ahhh…!

I strongly condemn your behavior. I strongly oppose your teaching methods. I strongly frustrated with your abuse of your power.

In fact, I'm disappointed with you. You had the power to lift us all. To empower us. To help us see that even if one student is different than the rest – that we should love them and respect them too. You had a great teaching opportunity and you MISSED it. Big time.

Kids are tender. I was freaking fourteen years old. I was tender, soft, easy to mold. And you, with your unwashed fingers, molded a part of my soul into not really loving myself.

I see the residues of your weak behavior in my system. I see how I am still afraid to seem feminine at times, just so I won't be caught by your unloving eyes. I see that I am afraid that I'm not manly enough, not according to your standards.

But let me tell you, love, that I am a man just as much as you. In fact, had I had to choose between being you or me, I would choose me.

I don't need to pester other people to feel important. I try to accept each and every person, no matter how much I oppose some sides in them. I don't have to put anyone down to feel better, and if I catch myself, then I apologize.

I am sickened by your unintelligent conduct. I am saddened by how messed up you were.

I am appalled by your inability to distinct between what's right and what's wrong.

And yet, with all of that, I choose to let you go.

I choose to let your memory go. I choose to wash away your disrespectful comments, your manic behavior. I choose to let it go.

Jacob, I look into your eyes and I see a damaged man. A damaged kid, who was not loved and accepted for what he was. I look into your soul and I see pain. I see anger and rage, and beneath it all I see pain.

I'm sorry I took your pain with me. This is your pain. All I can do is show you love.

Yes, I'm still a little afraid of you. But I choose to show you love, to send you love and healing. I understand that if you knew better, if you were more aware of yourself, and of your own pain, you wouldn't have done what you did.

I know that had you known better, you would have empowered me. You would have told me how great I am. You would have never implied that I am transparent, but instead told me that my light shines so bright, it impinges your eyes.

You would have told me that I am great. That I will go far in life. You would have told me I should take my time and experiment with girls and boys and not worry about anything, let my whole self come forth.

You would have told me, had you been bigger and stronger, that you see great talent in me. That I bring my whole self to the stage, and that you cannot stop yourself from loving me and wishing the best for me.

I would have appreciated that.

Jacob, I choose to release you, for once and for all. You have no dominion over me. You hold no authority over me. I am now, officially, in this moment, let you go.

I hereby forgive you for all of your wrongdoings.

More so, I forgive myself. I forgive my 14-years-old self for having given you the power. I forgive myself for not seeing through your feigned and known that you too are scared and afraid inside.

I forgive myself and embrace myself for not knowing that you were wrong. That being a true man means not to act in a certain machoistic way, but to act in a way that is authentic and congruent for each person.

I choose to love all men, all people, machoistic, gentle, manly or feminine. Above all, I choose to love myself, my whole self.

Finally, Jacob, well, let me thank you. I thank you for giving me this experience. Through this experience I learnt so much about myself and about life.

I thank you for teaching me that sometimes being in position of authority can make people a little drunk with power and out of line. It's a good lesson to know, and feel pity for them for not being able to avoid the toxic elements that may come with power.

I thank you, Jacob, for doing this to me at such a young age, while I was still so impressionable. It made me realize, through my own experience, just how tender a teenage soul is.

I thank you, Jacob, for opening me up to emotions of self-loathing and self-hatred. While I do not intend to use them, I am thankful for having experienced them, and for having the 'contrast' to know what I want to feel instead: self acceptance and self love.

I thank you, Jacob, for saying that I'm transparent. In many ways, I've tried to defy your statement and your prophecy. I have worked hard and labored much to achieve things I hold dear to my heart. It may be that your statement have actually pushed me to go further in life.

I thank you, Jacob, for choosing me of all people in the class. I would have felt really bad for any other student had you picked them for your exhibition of your self-loathing. I thank you because I could endure it. I did.

I thank you, Jacob, for instilling a secret feeling within me, that if someone is picking on me, that they might be jealous. I thank you for making me understand over the years that when people pick on others it's out of their own demons and self-hatred. I thank you for this valuable lesson.

I thank you for teaching me what it feels when someone doesn't accept you for who you are. Through this feeling of being rejected by you, I developed a hunger to make everyone feel included and loved. And this hunger drives me to work, lead, speak, write. I thank you for instilling this hunger in me.

I thank you for teaching me that I should never, NEVER give someone else the power over me. It took me many years to understand it, but I now do. I feel pity for you, and I choose to feel pity over every person who made me feel bad as a mean to bring themselves pleasure. I see through that. I thank you for helping me to see through that.

I also wish to thank you for knowing when to stop – I do believe, now that I see your own wounds, that you could have carried on, and damaged me even more. I appreciate that you did stop when you did. I bet it took some courage.

I wish to now express the words of the child in me. I wish to take the mask off of me, literally, and to tell you, "man, I feel so sorry for you, I feel pity for you. Look at you, surrounded by kids, and for you to feel better about yourself, you choose to put one of them down? Man, that's so sad. I'm really sorry for you. I send you healing and love. I feel your pain."

I apologize to myself for having given you, you little poor you, the power over me. What a mistake. I shall never let anyone have power over me. I shall know the truth, in which we are all equal, and we are all one. I release you from my dominion, and am willing to accept you only when your intentions are pure.

I apologize to myself. I love myself. I forgive you, Jacob. I see your pain. I do love you. I'm sorry for having judged you all these years – sorry for me, and sorry for you. I thank you for all that you have given me. May you be well, live a long and happy life, and heal all your inner wounds. Amen.

"Darkness cannot drive out darkness; only light can do that. Hate cannot drive out hate; only love can do that."

—Martin Luther King, Jr.
American minister and civil-rights activist

"You wanna fly, you got to give up the shit that weighs you down."

—Toni Morrison
American novelist, editor, and activist

LETTING GO OF SECRETS

We are entering one of the most important chapters in this book. Secrets.

But before we do, let's close down what we went through in the last two chapters about forgiveness. We understood that when we hold grudges and resentment, we are actually hurting ourselves; that through forgiving we are sending ourselves free. I then took you through a long process in which I had an inner dialogue, a sort of a letter, through which I led myself to forgiveness.

I cannot stress enough how much I'd like for you to do this process yourself. You may need to forgive your mother, your father, your ex-spouse, your child, your best friend, your teacher – and through that you will not let them off the hook, but you will release yourself of all that weight.

Please contemplate doing it. Take some time and write such a letter to one of the people you hold resentment against. You don't need to give it to them

– it's the writing process that matters, whether they are still alive or have deceased.

It is powerful, it is worth the time, and it liberates you. It helps you in turn to love yourself more. Which is why you are reading these lines.

Another HUGE tool that helps liberating you is the tool of letting go of secrets.

Secrets weigh us down. I'm no expert on the subject, but I do really appreciate it – as it's one of the subjects people least like to speak of.

You will find thousands of books about success and about relationships – and only few about shame, guilt and secrets.

Of the few, I think it's worth while mentioning Brené Brown's work – her books are absolutely liberating for me, and have given me much of the needed vocabulary to facilitate my own personal growth into becoming a better and stronger me.

Brown recommends only sharing your secrets with a person that you value, respect, and you know that they will not judge you, and that they will accept you even of what you did that you are ashamed of.

Let me share a secret with you. It's a secret that has weighed me down for years and years. And now I'm willing to let it go.

In my youth, as you may have understood, I had some confusion about my sexuality. I had a girlfriend at the age of 13, and she was marvelous and sweet – we had great few first sexual experiences together, kissing, making out, even experiencing first orgasms.

Yet at the time I had a dream that really confused me, of me and another older, imaginary boy, in the shower together. And it was pleasant.

When I told it to my girlfriend, Naomi, she was distort. "You know what it means, don't you?" she asked with her eyes widened.

"No..." I said.

"It means you are GAY," she said and began crying.

I cried to. I think.

We were thirteen.

But what was so odd was that I loved her a lot, and was attracted to her, I could feel that very clearly in my pants. But, Naomi was a very smart girl. So I guessed she was right.

Few months later our relationship ended, mostly because I felt she was very jealous and rather controlling (this pattern was to reemerge several more times in my relationships until I broke it piece by piece in my mid twenties).

Anyhow, we broke up. I moved to a new school, this fancy art school, in which there were quite a few students openly identifying themselves as gay. Good, I thought, time to experiment and SEE.

Neil, one of the kids in the class, was one of the most outspoken gay people. We began talking, and eventually Neil spent the night in my family's apartment. We kissed. It was weird, exciting, frightening.

Given all I heard and sensed about gayness, was both scared and thrilled. It was forbidden, it was for grown ups only.

But it didn't develop into a relationship. Neil was nice, but I couldn't see us actually... dating. Few weeks later I hit it off with another girl from class, and we became a couple. Her name was Dinah (all names made up of course to protect people's privacy and enable me to speak FREELY).

Now, Dinah and I were together for nearly two years, all through the ninth and tenth grade. We didn't sleep together, but we did everything else we could. It was great. It was a true love, big love. Fond memories.

Then we broke up and there came a year of experimenting. Been with few girls. Had my first sex, with someone I didn't love, and it was l-o-u-s-y. The furthest think from what I had expected. Made me think that possibly I was gay after all? I then had another encounter with a guy. And it was really good, actually.

Meantime, of course, I told nobody. My older brother David, who knows everything, told me that gay people are sick, and that it is really scary to be hit on by one. He was hit on by one in a party, and boy, was that scary or what!

I then travelled to Canada at the age of 16 for two years. There I experimented with a girl, then a boy. I was sure I was gay, but found it quite disappointing with this one guy. Tried it again in Israel with another guy - was even worse.

Then came along Rebecca, and became my girlfriend, and later, for a limited time, even my fiancé. We were together from my late teens into my twenties. Then came few serious relationships (as you can see I'm a serious relationship kind-a-guy), until I found Hallel, and now we are married and support one another in our lives' journey.

Why did I take you and I through the trouble of my romance and sexual escapades? I'm actually a very private person, so it ain't easy to write this.

The reason is that for me, this information is classified under the "never share, never tell" file cabinet. Due to much cleaning labor, I have cleaned this cabinet over the past few years. This is one of the only files left. I can't see any other files currently.

Yet this file - boy, it paralyzes me! Even as I write these words I'm a little sweaty.

I did tell it to Hallel from early on in our relationship, and she has been extremely supportive. She even said that it made me who I am. And that I shouldn't hide it.

But I kept hiding it from the world.

You see, to you, the fact I've been with boys, men, for few times in my teens may seem like "OK, where's the secret?"

But to me the fact that I have been with BOYS for FOUR times in my teens is just... HIDE and NEVER TELL kind of thing.

Let's put things into context. I was born into a religious and ethnic tradition of thousands of years, that basically denounces any one of my experimentations as "SINS". Like, sins-sins.

It's a SIN.

And I have tons of religious friends. In fact, I myself find my religion very intriguing. I freakin' wrote a book about it.

Also, I have many religious Christian friends, and many religious Muslim friends. To them too, this is a SINNNNN.

I hate to think that I have sinned.

Now, in my head, I don't see it as a sin anymore. I have many gay friends too, and I actually admire those who are openly gay.

As to me, I feel that if there was a line, a continuum, between being totally gay or totally straight, I would be somewhere in the middle leaning towards the straight. I do find women, personally, more attractive. But I find men attractive too.

I explained to Hallel early on (in fact, to myself too), that being able theoretically to go both ways does not mean I'm going to actually do something about it. I fell in love with her as a person, and I'm not going to cheat, either with a man nor with a woman. I'm quite monogamous, actually one of the most monogamous people I know (in serious relationships since freakin' age 13).

Back to the secret thing. Being told what I was told

by my brother, being often taunted in my youth for being gay (what can I say, I do have some feminine aspects that I don't want to hide by playing a the role of a jarhead when I'm not). Being told throughout my life that I SHOULDN'T even THINK of same-sex stuff – this has been the reality in which I experimented.

Difficult. At least for me.

I wanna be liked. I really do. By writing these words, by revealing this secret, I know that some will be drawn closer, due to my authenticity and humanity, while some will be drawn further, due to their judgment of what I did as "wrong".

I don't want to push anyone further away.

Especially, I don't want to push any person who is close to me away. What will my brother say? And my religious teacher?

"Listen," they may say, "it's ok that you did it, you've mistaken. But to then write about it?"

I want to write about it. I want to not have secrets weigh me down. I find myself as a highly moralistic person, with strong values and ideals. And ideally, I don't think any of us should walk around carrying secrets.

Not that I think you need to take your secret and share it with the world like I'm doing now. No. That's my journey. You should have your own, whatever feels liberating for YOU.

Studies have found that sharing a secret with only

one person helps taking away the negative side effects of having a secret.

What are these side-effects, you may ask. Well, let's have a look at that.

A 2015 research entitled "Exploring the secrecy burden: Secrets, preoccupation, and perceptual judgments", which was published in the Journal of Experimental Psychology, uncovered through four different studies that keeping a secret makes you feel weighed down — literally — and even limits your ability to get things done.

"Spending effort to keep your secret leads you to feel like you have less effort and energy for other tasks, and so they seem more challenging", the researcher, Dr. Michael Slepian, wrote. "This is the same kind of outcome we see when people are carrying physical burdens."

What's the fix? The researchers found that revealing a secret eliminated the negative effects that harboring a secret can have.

"When you talk about your secret, you start thinking about it constructively — processing it, making sense of it, learning how to cope with it — reducing your preoccupation with that secret and taking you off the path of burden," Slepian wrote.

But what if your secret simply CAN'T be revealed? Well, the research recommends "simply writing the secret down could still mitigate its negative effects."

And I want to add, find someone who you can trust, and ANY secret can be revealed.

There is a great relief in revealing secrets. It makes you waaaaay lighter. Jack Canfield says that hiding a secret is like being in the water, and trying to hide a beach ball under the water. The beach ball wants to go up, and by you pressing it down you are really tiring yourself.

I still need to do some processing regarding this secret of mine. But I've decided that life isn't worth living if I can't simply be myself. And if some people will walk away from me because they know I've been with guys – then, let them walk away from me. I want only people that love me AS I AM, accepting me AS I AM, and by that echoing my own love towards myself – AS I AM.

"To design the future effectively, you must first let go of your past."

—Charles J. Givens
American financial educator and author

"Accept yourself as you are. Otherwise you will never see opportunity. You will not feel free to move toward it; you will feel you are not deserving. Accept yourself as you are."

— Maxwell Maltz
American surgeon and author

THROUGH THE LOOKING GLASS

Loving yourself is something that requires work. You need to unlearn much of the crap you learnt and adopted along the way. And you need to relearn lots of good stuff that you have forgotten.

I watch little kids carefully. From the moment they understand how mirrors work, and once they've realized the figure in there is themselves, children tend to smile, laugh, giggle, even become embarrassed – all by the figure in the mirror.

Whereas I also watch adults carefully. When a person does not think you are looking, they tilt their chin upwards (do it now with me): they tilt their chin upward, squint their eyes gently, and look for flaws in their face. They raise their eyebrows (do it now!), open their eyes widely to look at the wrinkles or makeup around their eyes. Sometimes they might even check there's nothing stuck between their teeth. How will they do that? They will open their mouth widely while tightening their jaw and teeth, and quickly look around.

Only few people end up being pleased with what they see. Those few people tend to smile or nod at the end approvingly. Those are people I try to learn from.

But we all, ALL of us, forget that inside of us there's a sweet little child. That child is very sensitive, observant, and mindful of every gesture. When you squint your eyes at them – they feel… judged. When you raise your eyebrows at them – they feel intimidated. When you open your mouth and show your teeth – well, they feel quite scared!

You may find this whole previous paragraph funny or amusing. It may be. But I'm dead serious. You see yourself in the mirror few times a day – how often do you smile to yourself? How often do you nod to yourself? Let me tell you that the few super successful people I know, who love themselves and are just the person you'd like to hang around with, actually do smile to themselves. They actually do nod agreeably to themselves. They actually do.

I want to invite you to do that. Really. No biggie – just a quick smile, here and there… will you be willing to try?

Remember, there's a child in there. That child longs for your validation, approval, consent, and more than anything – your love. Smile when you look at yourself. Make sure not to leave the mirror, the bathroom, that sink or that window, before you smile a grateful smile to yourself.

"I used to look in the mirror and feel shame, I look in the mirror now and I absolutely love myself."

—Drew Barrymore
American actress, author and director

"Love yourself first and everything else falls into line. You really have to love yourself to get anything done in this world."

—Lucille Ball
American actress, comedian and producer

ADORING YOUR BODY

"Adoring your body" – now this may sound a little too much for you, possibly. But this is one key element to loving yourself. When you love your whole self, that includes your body too.

Yes, those wrinkles too. That weight, too. The chin, the nose, the big toes, the hairy parts, the not big enough boobs, the too big-a-boob, those saggy parts, the look of your penis (not to mention the size), the facial hair and those zits, the color of your eyes, your hair (should have been different of course), etc. etc. etc.

I personally struggled with several things. First, my nose. Felt WAY too 'Jewish' to me. Felt big. Then, those moles, skin-tags and other wonderful presents. Especially those moles with hair coming from them – why did you choose to strike your root here, hair, and why so freaking dark? And why in the middle of my face? Even before I began shaving I began clipping my mole's dark black hair. Splendid!

Then there were those eyebrows, growing one into the other. My girlfriend in my teens (are you holding tight?) actually plucked the middle between my eyebrows with those freakin' tweezers. Oh man.

Then there are other parts that received my undivided attention. That is, negative attention. I thought (and still think at times) I have too big of a butt. Yeah, I know it's a girl's problem usually – but girls, you don't have the monopoly over that one. I love dancing, and sometimes when I see my butt in mirror or in a video I cringe.

Sigh.

Also, as weird as it may sound, I have issues with my toes. Yep. I can never make them feel and look clean enough. In the summer I'm a little embarrassed walking with sandals. Oh yes.

Listen, I know my trouble may seem small to you, but it ain't for me. At least, it wasn't.

Few years ago I did an exercise in the bathtub, in which I began appreciating each and every part of my body. I also apologized to parts of my body that I judged.

It looked more or less like that:

Oh my forehead, my lovely forehead. How I have judged you over the years. I'm so sorry, really. (stroking the forehead) I really didn't mean to unappreciated you. Truth is that I relay appreciate you. So manly and tall, beautiful. Beautiful. And how you keep this brain of mine working so well behind you, you protect it, keep it safe. I appreciate that. I love you, forehead.

Oh my eyebrows, oh poor eyebrows, how much have I mistreated you! First, let me apologize for the tweezers thing, for me not having enough self confidence to tell Danielle not to pluck you middle hairs out. I'm really sorry. Then, also, let me apologize for years of wishing you were different, thinner and restricted. I'm sorry for that. I really appreciate you – giving me such a beautiful frame, accentuating my face, protecting my eyes from dust and all kinds of storms... I like how you serve as a couture line to my eyes, in a way making them look bigger. I appreciate you.

Oh eyes of mine. Poor eyes. How much of a hard time I had given you. No, you're not too small. No, your color is not blah or average – you are stunningly beautiful. Do you hear me? Stunningly beautiful eyes! I'm sorry for thinking you were too small and shoved under my eyebrows. I'm sorry for criticizing your performance, for lamenting constantly and complaining about your nearsightedness. Oh, I'm really sorry. Truth is that will all the work I have commanded you to perform, all the books I forced you to read even when you were tired, the driving, the watching, everything – you are miraculous. Really miraculous. I love you and I appreciate everything that you are doing for me. I love that you see in full color, that you enable me to enjoy the visual magnificence of this world. I appreciate you so much!

Nose, oh nose, dear nose of mine. I'm so sorry for giving you a hard time, thinking you are too big. Even being embarrassed of my 'Jewishness'. I love you and appreciate you. You rock, nose, you do. You are so heroic, and grand, and royal-looking. I love that you are so strong and manly. I also love how you remind me of my heritage and my lineage. I feel like my ancestors are with me when I look at you. Thank you for making me proud of who I am, and not giving up on me even when I demanded you to shrink. I want you to do nothing but being yourself.

Nostrils, oh nostrils.

Now, do you all get what I was doing?

I know you may want to read more, possibly in the future I'll write a "love your body" book, and we'll go into depth there. But for now there's nothing else you need, really, before you can do this exercise yourself.

Of course it makes you embarrassed. What the heck, this whole book should make you feel uncomfortable. What am I writing it for??

Do this. Do this with your whole body. Here's an example of how I spoke to my butt:

Butt, oh butt. Such a sweet butt. You always loved me, and I showed you so little love. I'm so sorry, really. Oh butt, my beautiful bottom. I want you to be exactly as you are. Big, round, jiggly, hairy – everything. You are one of my best companions. I practically sit on you so many hours of the day. So happy you are so cushie and comfy! Really, you are just the perfect perfect size.

I'm sorry for not appreciating you and wanting for

you to change for all these years. I love your presence, the statement you make. Seriously, you kick-ass (haha). You are a work of arse! (OK, I'll stop). I'm sorry for making you the butt of my jokes...

I love you butt, please keep being as you are, I love every little hair on you, how you move and jiggle, how you help me relieve myself of poop so graciously. You rock. I love you.

OK, I hope this wasn't too much TMI (TMTMI?) but I wanted to make the point clear: each and every part of your body deserves your appreciation.

When you appreciate your body, you may find that your body is actually answering to you. At least for me. My eyebrows said about the tweezers: "Yeah, it hurt you mother-f****r!"

Even the hair on my shoulder (yeah, I got that one going in my late twenties. "Recent edition!") – even the hair there told me, "why do you think we popped here? We are like epaulette of honor, and you have mistreated us! Wear us like a badge of honor, you are a true man now!"

So if your body speaks to you, let it speak. And respond.

If you feel uncomfortable, that's good. That's the way. I promise you that if you'll do this exercise every three months or so, your self esteem will change dramatically.

I don't care how much you weigh. You can

appreciate yourself. I recently finished reading Whitney Thore's "I Do It with the Lights On: And 10 More Discoveries on the Road to a Blissfully Shame-Free Life." It was great to read how a person weighing 378 lb. (171 kg) can be so confident and love herself. It was inspiring for me too, personally, and made me determined to love myself even more.

I don't care how physically disabled you are. You are perfect as you are. Even if your legs are weak, even if you are 'deformed' in some way. There's no such thing as being 'deformed'. Only 'beautifully formed.' Nick Vujicic, that amazing no-arms and no-legs dude, says "I don't believe I'm disabled. Yes, I have no arms and no legs but big deal. Doesn't matter how I look. It's who I am and what I do."

Be inspired. Love yourself as you are. Show love to your body. Please, show love to your body. Your body deserves it. It longs for it. And you are the only person that can give it the appreciation it craves for.

"Whatever God or whatever higher power you believe in, they brought us to this earth in a perfect way, and you have to learn to love yourself. Otherwise, it's an exhausting way to be."

—Callie Thorne
American television and movie actress

"I have a choice. I can be angry about not having limbs, or I can be thankful that I have a purpose. I chose gratitude."

—Nick Vujicic
Australian evangelist and motivational speaker

TAKE EXTREME MEASURES

You have to do whatever it takes to imprint on your mind that you love yourself. I've taken some extreme measures to do so. I want to share some of these with you. Hopefully you'll be a little extreme too!

But first, though it sounds silly, let's think for a moment on WHY. We've been talking all throughout this book on HOW. But why should we love ourselves? Why should I have taken extreme measures to convince my mind that I DO love myself?

Well, I think it's simple, and no need to make it complicated: when we love ourselves we get to do more, have more, and be more. Think of two people going to a casino. One person has only four tokens, those small discs used in lieu of currency in casinos. The other person has 400 tokens.

Who is going to have more chances to win? Who is going to do more playing and having more fun? And who is going to be ultimately happier?

Now, there is no straight answer. And sure we can

say that there are some benefits to having only four tokens. But generally, personally, if I had to choose, I'd choose the latter – 400 tokens please!

Just to get it out of the way – I'm not into casinos or gambling, in fact I pretty much oppose the whole thing.

But it's a great metaphor.

I think that SELF-LOVE is the token we play with in the casino called LIFE. The more self love we have, the more ability we have to dare, play more, have more fun, do more, and ultimately become more.

Self-love to me feels like a cushion. It helps us fall unto something soft whenever we do fall. And we fall ALL the time. Falling may be negative criticism. If we have enough of a 'cushion', enough of self-love, it wouldn't hurt as much.

There's this great quote by American author Elbert Hubbard: "To avoid criticism, do nothing, say nothing, and be nothing."

I like it. It's powerful.

In life we simply CAN'T avoid criticism. Especially when we want to do SOMEthing, say SOMEthing, and be SOMEone. When we want to claim our share in the universe, we WILL face criticism. And the only way I found to deal with criticism is to have a pretty cushie and comfy and feathery cushion of self love to fall on.

So this is what we do in this book: we increase our numbers of tokens, we add feathers (synthetic if you wish!) to our cushions.

If someone asks you why you liked this book, you can tell it explained you a lot about casino tokens and cushion feathers. ;)

Alright. Now to the real deal. Here are some of things I've done to increase my amount of self-love tokens, and add to my cushion of love to myself.

I wrote a long letter to myself explaining to me why I love myself. Why I'm sorry for being mean to myself some times. And why I am committed to love myself more and more.

I wrote a love poem to myself. Yeah.

I took as many photos of my childhood as I could find and hung them EVERYWHERE. The reason: I think children should receive love. Every child. Should adults...? Well, whenever I'm cynical or negative, I am not sure adult should all receive love. Therefore, whenever I bump into a picture of myself, age three, five, seven, I feel positive emotions toward that boy. And that makes me feel better. I want the best for him, meaning that I want the best for me.

Now, why do I say that I have taken things to extreme measure? Cause my office, aka my 'man cave', has pictures from floor to ceiling. I don't host anyone in my office, Hallel can actually not enter without my consent. Yep, I'm crazy. But I think Virginia Wolf was right when she had demanded an author should have "a room of one's own."

Basically I have my own floor, at the bottom of the house, for which I pay rent separately from my lovely income from my books and my art – and this place is my studio, my office, my heaven. And the pictures constantly remind me that I am loved, and that I'm worthy of love.

What else do I have in this shrine of mine to which NO friend has entered? Well, basically, anything that makes me feel proud. Here, I'll look around and I'll tell you: here's a certificate from age 13 of me graduating a one week course in surfing, and winning the third place at a competition in the end.

The reason I put it up is that in the beginning of that week I was the lousiest of all the 15 kids who were there. Through practice and perseverance I managed to slowly improve, and by the last day the kids who were not even considering me as 'competition', began rethinking!

It reminds me that I am capable of anything I put my mind to.

Then there are many photos on the wall, childhood, romantic relationships that helped me grow, friends from high school, from college (only those that I felt loved me and appreciated me).

Here's a badge that I put on my shirt, saying "Jonathan – Supervisor." I had this grand art project in Africa, had to have four workers I oversaw. We did a huge floor mosaic, sculptors, etc. And I had the most awful boss who oversaw the whole project, and gave me a really hard time.

I called Hallel several times from Africa and cried and cried over the phone. But eventually we finished the project, after less than four weeks. And I got the MONEY and it was GOOD. And this "Supervisor" badge reminds me that I can survive the most adverse circumstances, with this hateful boss who probably didn't get laid for too long.

Moving along the wall I see a greeting card I like from my friend Holly: "Jonathan – thank you for being such a central part of my journey this year. I love you! Holly".

I like this card, it makes me feel that I am loved.

Do you get the point? I hang diplomas, certificates, letters, cards, grade sheets, sketches, old calendar pictures that I like, even ATM slips that indicated that I just deposited a fat check. I have the tickets indicating I went to a Joel Osteen "Night of Hope" event (so proud of myself to have gone!) and the pamphlet of a Jack Canfield full year course for trainers (which I attended and graduated OMG!), and my most precious things, or at least some of the most precious things are little notes from Hallel, may it be for my birthday, or just a quick note she scribbled: "Jon love, you are so amazing for have done the dishes! Thanks and a kiss!"

Now, what if you don't have the ability to allow yourself the privacy of your own 'mac-cave' or 'a room of one's own' or that you are just embarrassed to actually take that space for you and you only? This is what I've done for the years BEFORE I got my office-cave. (All this and more – in the next chapter!)

"Privacy is not a rejection of those you love; it is your deserved respite for recharging your batteries."

—Wayne Dyer
American philosopher and self-help author

"If you do not love yourself, well, you cannot do anything well, that's my philosophy."

—Nawal El Saadawi
Egyptian feminist writer and activist

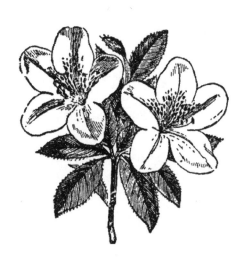

CAPTURING YOUR SUCCESSES

Basically, to continue the last chapter, we are all for enlarging our amounts of tokens, or of cushion feathers.

Lone before I had my man-cave I created a power-point presentation with my successes. Now, you don't have to be tech-savvy or anything. When smart-phones came out, I basically did much of it using the phone.

So. What is it exactly.

It's a folder or a power point presentation, in which you put all your photos or other things (soon to be explained) of things that make you feel good, accomplished, celebrated, loved.

In the power-point presentation I simply took photos of my old photos from my childhood (no need to scan or overdue it. Phone photos are FINE!). I added photos from recent time that I liked.

I also added few photos of landscapes that brought

me a feeling of ease. The talented photographer for all these photos is called Images. His given name is Google. Look for him. He's pretty versatile. He also got his own website, images.google.com. He has taken millions of photos, I don't know how he does that. Anyway, as long as it's for your own use, Mr. Google is happy for you to take any photo and... Voilà!

The reason I'm being slightly whimsical here is that we all have such amazing photos at our fingertips. And they let our soul loose and our heart sing. And if you put them in your own phone folder, and look at them often, you FEEL better.

Apart from my own photos and photos of landscapes, babies and other things that make me feel good, I began to DOCUMENT my successes.

For example, my friend Chaya saw a painting of mine in a home in Germany. She hurried to take a photo and to tell me: "One day I wanna have one of your works too!"

Now, instead of letting this moment of small victory vanish into the abyss of my email archive, I snapped a photo of my screen.

You can do it on your computer (search for the printscreen key on your keyboard), on your phone either press and hold the power and volume down buttons at the same time until your screen flashes (for androids) or press simultaneously the home button and the Power-off-on button located on the opposite edge of the phone.

Do it now, so that you know you can do it.

Now, all your screenshots will find their way into a screenshot folder. It's as easy as that.

Here's what I have in my screenshots folder on my phone: an inspirational quote by Nick Vujicic I saw and wanted to remember (by now you understand I'm a quote-addict right?); my sister's photo of a painting of mine in a gallery in Tel Aviv; a photo of my two nieces (they are adorable, really); a photo of my hard-working friend abroad with his wife smiling (I convinced him to go!); a Facebook message from my friend Judy saying I'm such an encourager and motivator, saying that "through your prayers and friendship I am motivated to be a better person" (aw shucks!); an e-mail from my Canadian friend Khursheed saying about one of my videos "Jonathan darling this is fucking amazing! Sorry there are no other words to describe it, I'm so impressed darling"; a Direct Message I got on Twitter from @jmmoore_62 "I am glued to your writings. I'm learning a lot!"; etc. etc.

Now, why is this important? Why am I taking your precious time, and precious trees of this earth to spend yet another paper? Well, because this is CRUCIAL.

You wanna have great successes in life? Begin by celebrating the tiny successes. Even before I had friends taking photos of my art abroad, or before I even had a Tweeter account, I understood that there are moments in life you MUST remember.

I have this friend, who texted me once after a long talk on the phone, "Jon, thanks for listening. You're a real friend."

I screen-captured it. It's important. When I feel down, to scroll through the photos in my screenshot folder, and see, "Jon, thanks for listening. You're a real friend"... - that's powerful. It makes me VALUE myself better, you see? Or sometimes my self esteem is low, and I think I'm writing to myself and that NO ONE will EVER read this BS cause it SUCKS. Yeah.

Then to see the Tweeter message of my friend June saying she's "glued" to my writing. Man, that feels good.

I want you to truly celebrate your successes. Someone left you a note, a kind note, in the office? Take a photo of it, then take a screen-shot so it finds its way to your screenshot folder. Then it's there. And while I clean my phone often, I never clean my screenshot folder. It's there for me.

You celebrated your friend's birthday and you like the photo of you? Screenshot. You went through your old files and saw something from years ago that made you feel "aww..." – Screenshot! You invested in buying yourself new shoes, and enjoyed the feeling of treating yourself as you looked at your feet – Screenshot!

How often should you look at your screenshot folder? Or, if you are computer savvy and prefer PowerPoint presentation?

As often as you can. I look at my photos once a day, in the morning. Sometimes when I wash the dishes I even put the photos as a slideshow. Yeah, you can do it on your phone too. The bottom line is that you want to inundate your brain with your successes.

Anyhow, without your effort, it will be inundated with crap and news and negativity. Your conscious effort to feed your mind positive images related to your self, your successes, your wellbeing – will pay back.

I promise.

And with time, you will FEEL better. You will walk into the casino of life with more tokens than before. And if you receive any nasty criticism, your cushion of self-love and self-esteem will comfort you when you get bumped and fall down.

You may think – yeah, but it's complicated, and too… technical for me. Well, you can do it hands-on, with a journal. Have a journal for your successes and triumph – only for those. And set it close to you and read through it often. It can have pretty awesome results.

Do it. Invest in yourself. Make your folder thick. Make your PowerPoint presentation heavy. Make your journal full. Make your love to yourself express itself physically in this world.

"Recall happy times from the past. Photos are a great memory-prompt, and because we tend to take photos of happy occasions, they weight our memories to the good."

— Gretchen Rubin
American author, blogger and speaker

"You can search throughout the entire universe for someone who is more deserving of your love and affection than you are yourself, and that person is not to be found anywhere. You yourself, as much as anybody in the entire universe, deserve your love and affection."

—Buddha
5th century BCE Indian sage and teacher

THE THREE ENEMIES INSIDE

Let's take a short break from all the technical how-to's and to-do's and "another good idea is…" and let's speak now of the worst enemy we all have.

You noticed by now, I'm a fairly positive person. I rarely focus intentionally on the negative stuff. But now I'm going to go off the path of goodie-goodies and talk about the dark trees off of the path.

I love trees. But these are DARK trees.

In them, there are DARK creatures. Creatures that if they GET YOU, you become their prey, you are devoured by them. They will eat each and every part of you, and leave nothing good.

Who are these dark forces, and who is their king?

These dark forces are self-loathing, self-hatred and self-criticism.

They are all PART of YOU.

They look like you, they behave like you. But you

MUST remember that these are dark forces that will EAT YOU ALIVE.

Self-loathing says: "*I don't like that you do this. You ALWAYS do this! You are soooo stupid!*"

Self-loathing awaits your failure, big or small. Right around the corner it jumps at you, and says, with a smile, "*you suck! You disgust me!*"

Self-loathing forces seem fair and OK, but you should watch for them. They are the ones that make you look at a photo and say, "*you look ugly here!*"

Yet self-loathing is nothing like Self-hatred. Oh no. Self-hatred makes Self-loathing look like an angle. Self-hatred is blatant. Self-hatred will wait for you, be really quiet, and just when you are really close, shout in your ear: "*I HATE you!*"

Self-hatred is more in-your-face than their friend Self-loathing. The forces called Self-hatred will look for your worst moment. You see them less than Self-loathing, but boy, when they come, you need to BEWARE. They can choke your soul to death. Run away from them when you smell them.

Unlike these two, the Self-criticism seems less appalling. Wearing an intellectual disguise, they will try and sound so matter-of-factly and so knowledgeable, that if you forget who you are talking with, you will easily fall into their trap. They are the forces that tell you, *"but you screwed up last time."* The Self-criticism forces tell you in a whisper, rather than in shouting: *"but you know that you are not GOOD enough"* and they whisper *"you don't deserve THAT!"*

Self-criticism will come at your moments of success. They won't come when you are down, oh no, why should they? They'll leave the work for two dumber ones, those Self-loathing and Self-hatred. Oh no. Self-criticism will see themselves as invited to your celebrations. They will come to the front of your mind, at the vortex of your perception and say: *"but this person doesn't REALLY love you. Wait till you need them, then you'll see."* They will hiss things like, *"Oh, that speech of yours was a little inadequate. No worries. You can screw up next time."*

The Self-criticism forces are smart, and you should watch for them. But they too, like the two other forces, work for the King of all forces. The dark king. The one with the mask.

"I'd become severely depressed in my thirties, and for almost a decade I spiraled down into paranoia, rage, self-loathing, and thoughts of suicide."

—Byron Katie
American self-help author and speaker

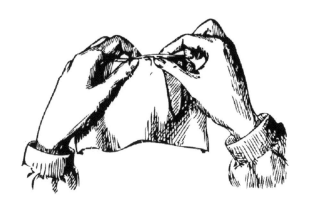

"Social media, despite its reputation as the ultimate agent of self-promotion, actually feeds on self-loathing."

—Meghan Daum
American author, essayist, and journalist

THE INNER-ENEMY
WITH THE MASK

No one is stronger or mightier than the King of all the inner dark forces.

He is the invisible King. You don't see him. He wears a mask that makes him seem like your best friend. Like an advisor. Like a true benefactor.

But don't be mistaken. The King knows very well what it does. Whereas his three subordinates come at moments of exercise, when it is time for them to come, the King, without you knowing, is ever-near you. This is what made him the King. He feeds on your soul more than the other three ever dream. Self-loathing is a baby next to the King. Self-hatred is an armature. Self-criticism is an ignorant deputy.

Don't worry, I'll reveal his face to you in a moment. Not that you will believe me. This is what the King of the dark forces is an expert in: making you think he's no biggie. He will tell you: "*Oh, what he says is bullshit, no?*"

The King of all your inner dark forces is not fear. It's not rage and it's not depression. These are important forces, but they don't strike as often and as severely as the King.

The King has his ways. He has his mask, so that you will NEVER recognize him. Take his mask off, and he vanishes. But he'll come back immediately with a new mask.

The King is Self-doubt.

Self-doubt?

How is Self-doubt stronger than Self-loathing, or Self-Hatred, or Self-criticism? How is he mightier than paranoia, fear, depression, rage, anger…?

Oh, he is.

Don't worry. You might be under his effects right now.

King Self-doubt has taught few things to the other forces, especially to Self-criticism. Self-criticism often knows how to sound like King Self-doubt. Self-criticism also employs a tone of speech that seems at time harmless. Self-criticism learnt from the King that in order to be constantly invited and never hushed away they must sound intelligent, wise, concerned for YOUR wellbeing.

But still, Self-criticism is only the deputy. Self-criticism do not have the power that the King exercises over you. It's the King that rules the Kingdom of dark forces, always wishing to expand it to every good soil in your ever-expanding soul.

The King has learnt the way through the guards. While often Self-criticism is thrown away through the gates of your mind's castle, the King knows how to remain always invited.

The King doesn't SEEM dark at all. The King is there FOR you, or so it seems.

The king also doesn't use such ignorant phrases such as the deputy, Self-criticism. While the latter may say, *"You screwed up! You always do it!"* the King will NEVER use such language.

Instead, the King speaks in soft-spoken words. His sentences are short. His tone always finishes with a question. The King of the dark forces tries to win your heart and take the place of your honored advisor, your Intuition.

The King has learnt to speak and sound like your Intuition. He has learnt that she speaks in short sentences, sometimes even without words. And so the King constantly tries to do the same.

Whereas Intuition tells you, "I feel you can do it!" the King only says, *"Mmmm…. Can you?"*

Whereas Intuition tells you, "It will help you shine" the King says *"Hopefully… it will be unfortunate if it won't, won't it?"*

The King likes you not to affiliate him with those other dark forces, his subordinates. He would like to be ever present in your castle. To ever advise you.

All that you have done in your life that was well, was because you DIDN'T listen to the King, to Self-doubt himself.

All that you have done in your life that did NOT go well, was because you DID listen to the King, to Self-doubt in all his glory.

Do I really need to give you examples? The relationships that didn't work? Intuition told you, "No, I don't have a good feeling." But Self-doubt asked, *"why, do you really think we may find someone better than that?"*

In your health and fitness, in your career, in your free time, in your finances, in ALL of your relationships, the King, Self-doubt, always struggles to undermine your efforts. He tries to sway you off from the path that is GOOD for you. He feeds on your energy going to HIM and to his Kingdom. He feeds on your giving energy to Self-loathing, to Self-hatred and to Self-criticism.

By exercising his well-crafted speech, his ever-gentle questions, his dance with uncertainty, his qualms of hesitation, the joy of having you stuck in indecision though you KNOW the right thing to do...

The King's powers are MIGHT. You don't even know when he's around, when he's speaking, when his dark energy begins to wrap your mind. You don't even need to go off the castle and wonder around the dark forest. You can remain well seated in your chamber, and Self-doubt, the King, disguised by true concern and love and care – will strike you ever so gently with dubiousness, suspicion, confusion – all to bring your mind to HIS Kingdom. Where he can FEED off of you.

When you have listened to more than one sentence of him, you are falling fast down the path of darkness. Your eyes blare, your mouth slows down. Even the voices of your dear Intuition drown by the King's loving embrace. *"Oh will it? Perhaps we shall wait? Perhaps this is asking for too much? Perhaps? Possibly? maybe?"*

Then you find yourself in a trance. It started by a simple question, seemingly well intended, caring one. But then you hesitated, didn't know what to answer, and the king hurried to tell you, *"Well if I remember correctly, last time you chose to do THAT, well, do I remember right? Was it not rather unsuccessful?"*

Then the more you listen to the King the more the voice of Intuition drowns and disappears. You don't even hear her nor feel her hand grabbing you, and you are led down the staircase by the smiling King, who whispers, *"You shouldn't, should you? You don't know, don't you? You don't want to, don't you?"*

And with each question you find yourself closer to the gates, leaving your beloved castle. You don't hear Intuition's whispers, her voice long gone, and the sound of your protective horses in their stables, their screaming and shouting for you not to leave, doesn't even register in your mind. And then you are out there, in the trail, when you hear Self-criticism joining behind you, saying: *"But you always mess up that way anyway"* and you see the wretched Self-loathing saying *"here comes the stupid one again, thinking that this time it's different, ha-ha!"* and Self-hatred, *"Why do you think you can even THINK of it as a possibility?! You pitiful, pathetic, sorry you!"*

And before long you are devoured, in the middle of

the dark forest, by the dark forces having a feast. Your energy is drained, your whole being is consumed by the dark forces.

To the outside world you can't explain what had happened. But you are tired, exhausted, depleted, emptied of all good.

And it's so weird, because you were actually optimistic.

To the outside world, to those who care about you, you can't even explain what happened. Truth is, that even to yourself you lack the words. You ask yourself indeed, "What happened?"

Little do you know that it was Self-doubt that seduced you, that took you out of your castle. Little do you know that you fell, yet again, to his seducing powers. Little do you know how he operated, how he sounded totally innocent. Little do you know what had happened to you.

All you want is OUT, to go to sleep, to drown yourself in food, in shopping, in porn, in drugs, in other outer expression of the inner feast taking place within you: the dark feast in which Self-loathing, Self-hatred, and Self-criticism feed on your soul, with the sad look of their King.

But there is a way out.

"Doubt kills more dreams
than failure ever will."

—Suzy Kassem
American film director and author

"When you doubt your power, you give power to your doubt."

—Honoré de Balzac
19th century French novelist and playwright

WINNING AND OVERCOMING SELF-DOUBT

OK, I think it's time for us to get clearer about how to win King Self-doubt. Then we can move on with our book. I don't want to give Self-doubt and his dark forces too much space in this book. But I do sense that this part is needed. So let's do it, and move on, shall we?

King Self-doubt cannot be killed. That's the first thing we need to understand. If you are saying "Kill the damned bastard!" you are not in the right direction.

Why not? Because you are emitting energy to him. He's getting your attention. He can then said, "Wow, you seem unhinged, don't you? It's not like you might think there's some truth in my words, right?"

And then you begin falling into his trap. He is smarter than you. Should I repeat this? He is smarter than you. He has access to your memory faster than your consciousness. He will prove you wrong, prove himself right, and do it all without much effort.

In fact, let's stress again the fact that he IS responsible to much of the unhappiness in your life. He IS your arch-enemy. And he CANNOT be killed, nor convinced, nor won over by plausible explanations.

Anything you SAY to him, any attempt to CONVERSE with him maturely, will give him the court advantage to blind you, impair your hearing, and put you to a trance in which HE is the leader and not you.

He is only WAITING for you to begin responding to him. That's what you've been doing. You've tried all of the methods you know in your adult life.

The only problem is that the King is PART of you. He knows ALL your arguments. He has been with you and watched EVERYTHING. And so, like in a worst nightmare, he can attack you again and again, and you WILL not win.

Am I making the point clear? The King, Self-doubt himself, WANTS you to respond to him. And you must NEVER do it.

NEVER respond to him.

The way to overcome the King is to first understand him.

In fact, though he is the King of the dark forces, it's worth understanding his story.

I once had a dog – it was a sweet sweet dog, that was owned by my girlfriend Rebecca. When we moved in together she brought her dog with her. Let's call him Genius.

Genius was a bichon frise dog, white, fluffy, chubby, the most adorable you can find.

Genius, however, had some difficulties.

He had skin soars, and to relieve his pain, he would chew on his skin soars. It would begin in licking. Seemingly, the licking was fine, as it was a natural thing to do. Then, Genius would continue to nibbling. The nibbling would release him of some of the pain, and would then lead to munching.

By then we'd say, "Genius!" and he'd look up, understand that he had done something wrong, and lay his head down.

No later than two minutes later he'd begin licking again. Then nibbling, munching, and actual guzzling. On his own skin. If we are in the other room or so, he'd keep eating until he'd hit some actual nerve or the bone or something (oh it hurts for me to write about it!), and then he'd yelp the most painful yelp you ever heard.

Poor Genius.

We tried everything. We tried creams, oils, putting medical gauze on his leg (he'd move it), wrapping his legs with various materials. Nothing helped.

When the veterinarian said, "It's getting worse," looking at the shiny red areas devoured on Genius' legs, we said, "We know!"

The veterinarian then said we'll have to use an

Elizabethan collar around his neck, this plastic cone thing to prevent him from licking himself.

In the following days poor Genius was moaning and groaning, as if we at least castrated him. His look was pitiful, he tried again and again to reach his legs, and we'd see the plastic cone banging all over.

Genius' look, whenever he looked at us, was resentful. His eyebrows were tight and he seemed disapproving of our behavior and of how we DARED to put the cone around him.

Oh how he liked when we took it off for him to eat actual FOOD rather than his own body. Then we'd run after him with the cone, and he'd run as fast as he could as if his life depended on it (which, no insult, wasn't too fast for our chubby Genius).

But week by week, the wounds began to heal, until eventually they healed completely.

We then took the cone off, and Genius was really happy.

But we kept the cone. And every time Genius began developing the beginning of such a wound, we'd immediately return the cone for few days.

So, how is Genius related to our Self-doubt, to that mighty and frightening King?

The truth is that there is more similarity than we may guess.

Genius didn't want to lead to his wounds growing worst. All he wanted was to lick them, in a way, to relieve the pain.

Similarly, King Self-doubt, as awful as he may have sounded, doesn't want, in his heart, for your inner wounds to grow worst. All he wants is to protect you, in a way, to relieve your future pain. To protect you from reliving the awful pain you have already experienced in the past.

Genius, though his name says otherwise, wasn't the smartest of creatures. Had he known that his licking would cause him more harm, would have refrained from it. But he was instead moved to agonizing self-inflicted terror, just because his brain couldn't comprehend the connection between licking, which seems to relieve the pain, and between his deepening wounds.

This is getting more and more profound. Do you bare with me? Go to pee or grab some bite to eat, I want you focused when you read this.

Similarly to Genius, the King, Self-doubt, doesn't KNOW that through voicing his legitimate concerns, he is going to inflict more pain on him. He doesn't know that doubt will lead to the wrong actions, which will create future suffering.

For example, though you really WANT to do something, you instead let the King to convince you that you really SHOULDN'T. Instead you choose to do something you don't REALLY want. In turn, the fact you don't REALLY want it, leads to a low commitment, low participation on your side. This, of course, lead to failure, or, in the best scenario, to mediocre results.

The King then tells you, *"remember that failure?"* or

"Those results were pretty mediocre, weren't they?" and his mere words lead you to be led by him, further and further down the spiraling staircase, led by Self-doubt, until you find yourself in the dark forest again.

What's so unique is that King Self-doubt does not really LIKE to be in the forest.

Seriously.

King Self-doubt is a more intelligent creature than his three forces. This is why he is the King, and they are his subordinates.

The King prefers the coziness of the Castle, being in the comfortable grandeur, than being in the cold forest seeing the stupid dark forces devour you and your energy.

When Genius used to yelp, after eating his skin out and creating the most frightening bright red sour, his face would seem so... sad. He really looked sad. I felt pity for him.

Yes. I know you understood. There, in the feast of the dark forces, out there in the dark forest, the King actually looks sad.

He'd prefer going back to the warm and cozy Castle.

There, in the woods, he is waiting for you to jump up and kick the three forces in the balls. Eventually you always do it.

Eventually you ALWAYS get up. It's your nature. Much like it's the nature of the King to lead you down the staircase and into the forest.

But WHY does the King do it? Why does he do it, if he LIKES to remain in the Castle?

You need to understand that whenever the King receives your ENERGY, he CANNOT do ANYTHING BUT put you in a trance, and lead you down the staircase. He doesn't have any other option. That's HIS nature.

Much like Genius doesn't have any other option than to munch on his wounds though it's not good for him, so cannot the King do anything else but lead you down, though it's not good for him either.

Let's move on. How do we therefore overcome the King?

First of all, now we have more empathy to the King. And that's good. It makes us realize that he has a role. He does.

There's a reason why the King can get into the Castle, and why his dark subordinates can't. The King was actually invited there early on. You NEEDED him. His words often protected you. Remember?

Remember when you were a kid, the King saved you from some stupid stuff. That's when your Intuition was still developing.

Over the years Intuition developed beautifully. It's true that she speaks quietly, that her words are reticent, that sometimes you can get frustrated and say, "But I can't hear you!"

But Intuition cannot raise her voice. He nature is a

delicate one. It's YOU that needs to silence the noise, so that you can LISTEN to her.

But more often than not you listen to the King. The King is a smart being. He's dumb because he doesn't know better than to kick himself –and you – out of the castle. But he is also smart because he learnt that there are many ways of speech to which you will NOT listen.

The King, Self-doubt, learnt that if he employs the speech of Self-criticism, Self-hatred and Self-loathing, you spot him in a second. You yell: "Stop it, Self-doubt!"

And aw, does that hurt the King or what. He thinks to himself, "But I'm a King. How can you SPEAK to ME that way?!?! And it was YOU who invited ME here in the first place!"

Then the King agonizes. All he wants is your attention and love. He does NOT want to be yelled at. He wants to stay in your castle, and for you to be really nice to him, invite him everywhere, feed him and nurture him. He DID serve you well many times. Your treatment of being ungrateful to him is indeed a wrongdoing on your part. Don't be ungrateful for those who helped you.

When you yell at him, when you kick him in the butt, that's when the King goes off to the corner, and begins rubbing his hands in one another. That's when his dark nature comes through. That's when he thinks of HOW to get your energy. He thinks of the BEST ways to get to you.

He did it before, and he will ALWAYS do it. Much like Intuition NEVER raises her voice and always speaks quietly, Self-doubt ALWAYS comes back with a better mask, to win you over again. It's HIS nature.

Which kinds of masks does the King have? Oh, wow, it would take me a whole book (not like this one, a BIG one), to even begin describing all his masks.

Sometimes he wears the mask of a caring mother. Or a caring father. Sometimes he wears the mask of an older lady, or a teacher. Sometimes he wears the mask of a baby, or a child. Sometimes his mask is the rational and slightly-remote professor, saying, *"I do doubt that this will work, but I may be wrong, even though I have never been wrong, not that I remember."* Yet other times he wears the cheerleader's mask: *"You can do it! You can do it! Just watch out not to get hurt, you do remember what happened last time, right?"* Other times he wears the doctor's mask: *"I do think it's better to rest, wouldn't you?"* and sometimes the partier's mask: *"Oh, you can have so much fun here, it means you are a fun person! Going away would mean missing on all the good stuff, and you don't want to miss all the GOOD stuff, right?"*

There are thousands and thousands, if not millions of masks that the King can employ and create in a second. Yet, my favorite mask is the mask of no other than…

"I don't have a good feeling about it, do you?"

You hear this gentle voice and you become alarmed. "Intuition?"

"I just don't know about this, you know?"

"Intuition? Is that YOU?"

"I would tell you if I had a good feeling, but I don't. But it's totally up to you, is it not?"

"Well, yes. But I want to hear your opinion, Intuition," you say.

"I think this might not be the best thing," you hear the whispering voice, "I really care for you, and I just don't have a good... hunch for that, do you?"

"I..." you say, "I...—"

"Why don't you just wait and see? No need to rush, right?"

"I... guess..." you say, and you don't even notice how your drowsy mind begins to speak slower and slower.

The rest is already clear.

Only later, in the woods, drained of energy and passion, emptied of hope and joy, there, do you realize what had happened.

"Self-doubt!" you shout, and look at the saddened King.

You kick off the three dark forces, who have brought their giant friends Paranoia and Depression over.

Everyone runs to the woods in fear. They see that you have HAD IT.

You look with anger at Self-doubt. You brush your clothes off, and walk back to the Castle.

Self-doubt, behind you, walks with his head bowed down.

Frustrated, you walk back through the gates. You nod to the disappointed horses, who bow their heads down. You climb up your magnificent Castle. You don't even remember going down this spiraling staircase.

Then you see Intuition, smiling, ever-calm, ever-loving.

"But," you say, "why didn't you SAY anything?"

She whispers, with a gentle smile, *"I did."*

"The only real valuable
thing is intuition."

— Albert Einstein
German-born theoretical physicist and activist

"Before you speak, it is necessary for you to listen, for God speaks in the silence of the heart."

—Mother Teresa
Albanian Roman-Catholic nun and activist

INTUITION

She is the most precious guest in your Castle. And you need to listen to her. She will direct you and guide you. She is your best source of intelligence.

For years we lived on the notion there is ONE intelligence. This was measure by Intelligence Quotient (IQ). Then we learnt that finding the IQ level of a person does not help solve many of our riddles, such as why some people are more financially successful than others, even though they have a lower IQ?

Then came Emotional Intelligence. Though the term first appeared in the 1960s, it took several more decades to be developed into something we all can speak without people bursting in laughter (like they did in the 1990s).

In the future, we will see another form of Intelligence receiving more and more attention. That is: Intuitive Attention. This is a form of intelligence that cannot be tracked by our old ways of measuring.

But it is true and strong, and the following years

will show it is REAL.

Currently, at the time of the writing of this book, the term Emotional Intelligence brings some 8 million results on Google. At the same time, the term Intuitive Intelligence brings only 400 thousand results. The term Intuitive Intelligence doesn't even have, as of now, its own Wikipedia article, while Emotional Intelligence has an exhaustive article, with over 100 references.

We live in an era in which the power of intuition slowly emerges in front of our eyes. Wait and see.

To come back to our allegory about your mind, about Intuition and King Self-doubt, your goal is to constantly quiet down King Self-doubt, and to listen to what Intuition whispers.

That is easier said than done. As we saw, the King can often SEEM, TALK and ACT as if he is Intuition herself.

But don't be fooled. He is easily discoverable.

If you ask your Intuition: "Is it you that speak, my Intuition?" she answers, "I am her."

If you ask your King, wearing one of his many masks, "Is it you that speak, my Intuition?" his answers ALWAYS end up with a question. He may say:

"Why are you asking? Let's focus on the decision at hand, and the decision does seem to me quite irrational, is it not?"

Or, when you ask, "Is it you, my Intuition?" you may hear the King trying to whisper:

"I am your bloody Intuition, I talk like her, I act like her, I even freakin' whisper, why would you NOT think it is ME?"

Soon you'll see that it is not your Intuition speaking.

The King can be EASILY exposed, as long as YOU remember to ask QUESTIONS.

By that you are using HIS sword, HIS drug, HIS trick.

"Is this YOU, my King Self-Doubt?"

"Why, why should you think it was me? And if it was me? Should you not focus instead on WHAT I'm saying rather than clinging to WHO said that? Does that seem smart? That's only another proof that you currently do NOT posses the ability to decide, is it not?"

Instead of answering to the King's questions, keep asking him, "Is this you, sweet King Self-doubt?"

"Well why is all this insistence on WHO is here rather than on WHAT I'm screaming? Is this not mere stupidity?"

The distinction can be made easily. Self-doubt feels attacked when he is confronted. Self-doubt only wants you to respond and fall into HIS trap. By asking him your OWN QUESTION you can easily see how his mask falls off.

Now, instead of exposing him and then throwing him up the window, and then having him enter the chamber again as one of the servants, as Intuition, dressed as a baby, or as a poor peasant – instead of you triggering him to start figuring his next move, just do the following. This can CHANGE your life, as long as you remember to do it:

"Oh sweet King, most loyal King, thank you so much for your input. You are SOOO valuable, and SOOO sweet and loyal…"

Now you will notice his mask-less face showing a hopeful look.

"Come," you say to him, "come and sit on me, near me, I want you up close."

Now he comes, ashamed but willing.

If you want to be really really smart, tell him, "I was just about to listen to Intuition, would you like to join me while I caress your head?"

Then you'll see the King nodding his head gently. Caress him. Love him. Embrace him.

Your King is good. His intentions are good. Yet he is unintelligent. He cannot develop the abilities that Intuition has. He cannot see clearly that the path in which you give HIM energy leads you BOTH out of the castle and into the dark forces hands.

So LOVE your King. Embrace Self-doubt. Spend time together doing what YOU love. Whenever he begins asking his doubtful questions about your abilities, about what you deserve and what you don't, about how awful it may be if you trust and then you get hurt… - whenever he does that, ask him:

"Oh, is it you, sweet Self-doubt?"

And then, without waiting for an answer, invite him closer again, "Come, love, sit here with me," and notice how he gets silence.

You may ask, "But, shouldn't I LISTEN to him sometimes? Doesn't his voice represents REASON or CAUTION?"

The answer here is clear. NO.

Reason or caution are parts of your Intuition's abilities. If you delegate to her all of the responsibilities that you supposedly give Self-doubt, you will soon hear her say things that will sound very much like Self-doubt, with a similar wording, but with a different source.

"I wouldn't hurry," you may hear her say, "I would wait and see how committed THEY are first."

Or you may hear her saying, "I don't want to go there. I don't want to go there."

If you develop and train your ear to listen well to her voice, you may hear that some sentences actually end up with an exclamation mark. "I don't want to go there!"

But you will never hear her giving you a question mark at the end. It's NOT in her NATURE.

Intuition is ever-knowing. If she doesn't know, she'll tell you, "I don't know right now. Let's sleep on it. I need to connect and gather more information."

But she will NEVER consult with you, or with any other HUMAN being. Your intuition is connected to Source, she is connected to God, connected all that has been, all that is, and to all that will ever be. She is connected to the shared intelligence of all humanity, of all reality.

Don't under estimate her. Underestimating her leads to suffering, to constant erring, to misfortune and to unhappiness. Adopting her, caressing her, listening to her, embracing her, taking care of her, nurturing her, being there for her, quieting it all for her, dedicating time to her, SEEING her – that's what you are now asked to do.

"My business skills have come from being guided by my inner self - my intuition."

— Oprah Winfrey
American media proprietor and philanthropist

"Intuition is a very powerful thing, more powerful than intellect."

—Steve Jobs
American technology entrepreneur and inventor

DUMPING GRATITUDE

Look, this subject has been hashed and rehashed over and over again. But I cannot leave without including it. This "subject" is Gratitude.

Now, there's a reason why I didn't title this chapter "Gratitude". With so many books, articles and mentions, we've become immune to the word and to its powers.

Similarly, with quite the opposite, the word "Terror" used to evoke real fear and actual terror within us. But with this word being on the news ALL the time, it slowly lost much of its inner weight and emotions attached. Not that we aren't afraid, we are, but we are not 'terrorized' as we were before by this word.

Similarly, the word "Gratitude" has lost somewhat from its weight. "Gratitude feels almost like a Hallmark card, like a quote you'll bump into, like yet another book in the Self-help section.

And nevertheless, like the word LOVE, even though it has been used so many times, it still holds GREAT powers.

Really GREAT.

So, allow me to try and re-structure this word in your head, will you? This will enable you to see this word in a fresh way, that might then drive you to actually enjoy the HUGE benefits this word carries with it.

The word Gratitude comes from the Latin root **grat**, meaning *pleasing* or *thanking*. Words from this root have something to do with being pleased or being thankful. To *in***grat***iate* yourself is to make others feel thankful for something you've done. To *con***grat***ulate* is to express how pleasing someone's success is.

Similarly, to feel **grat***eful* is to feel thankful, or to feel the pleasure for something. **Grat***itude* is a feeling of thankfulness or of pleasure.

I want us to divert from the "Gratitude as thankfulness" mode, in which we all operate, and shift to the "Gratitude as pleasuring" mode, in which only the super-successful people operate.

You see, when Oprah Winfrey speaks of her gratitude journal, she speaks of it not as if it was a mere tool of noting thankfulness, but as a tool to tool of noting PLEASURE. She writes what brought her PLEASURE throughout the day, rather than what she is merely "grateful" for.

I know it may sound like a small difference, but this small difference can be life changing.

Gratitude is currently affiliated for many of us with a list of things that we SHOULD do. There's an undertone of reprimand in the word gratitude, as it often comes along with the word SHOULD in the same sentence: "You should be GRATEFUL that we have this 'boring' food on our table!" or "I know I should feel gratitude for this present I got from him, but all I feel is sheer disappointment."

Yes. Gratitude to many of us holds a religious-should-obligation-must-to-do's-expected-required kind of attitude. And this CANNOT work as a mean to LOVE yourself.

But nevertheless, the concept of gratitude is one of the most important concepts there are. It CAN change your life. It DOES shift your mind from a mentality of scarcity to a mentality of 'more than enough'. It's really powerful.

And this is why we are now to relearn this concept, in a way that sticks, in a way that you will find pleasure in.

"Take your pleasure
seriously."

—Charles Eames
American designer and architect

"For years I've advocated keeping a gratitude journal, writing down five things every day that brought pleasure and gratefulness"

—Oprah Winfrey
American media proprietor and philanthropist

AMPLIFYING YOUR WORDS

What we are learning can really sound foreign and almost sacrilegious to those of you hard-working-puritans-perfectionists-to-do lists type of people.

But I care for you.

So I'm not going to give up on you.

I'm going to try and prove to you, in this chapter, that you should seek PLEASURE in your everyday life.

I'm not saying that you should stop doing what you are doing and going carelessly after lusts of the moment. I DIDN'T say that.

What I did say, dear, is that you MUST find TONS of pleasures in your day to day life, if you want to be happier. Finding these moments is a MUST, and it's a sign to your subconscious that you LOVE yourself.

So let's look into that – finding pleasure in your

every day life.

If we look at the previous quote, by Oprah Winfrey, we see that Oprah is advising to write down "five things every day that brought…"

Look at the EXACT wording. What's the word?

Yep. PLEASURE. Also, "gratefulness." But pleasure comes FIRST.

Why is it that we are so INTIMIDATED by this word, "pleasure"? It sounds almost like a sin.

But this is what life is to be about: pleasure. Pleasure!

Speaking of Oprah, it's no coincidence that her favorite Bible verse is Psalm 37:4: *"Delight yourself in the Lord, and he will give you the desires of your heart."*

I love this verse. The word "Delight" is a very powerful word.

Yet in today's world we are a little afraid of such STRONG words as "delight" or "pleasure". We much prefer "enjoy" or "OK" or "cool".

But, speaking of the Bible (atheists, bare with me just two more verses!) it also says that "Death and life are in the power of the tongue." (Proverbs 18:21) Now, in Hebrew, the word 'tongue' is the same word as the word: "wording."

Now, let's re-read the sentence: "Death and life are in the power of the WORDING."

If you chose your wording WISELY, then the rest

of the verse goes that you shall *"eat the fruit thereof."* The previous verse in Proverbs, just one before the famous Death and life verse, states that "with the increase of his lips" so shall a man "be filled."

The point I'm trying to make is that your WORDING counts. And if you choose your wording well, your life will become WELL. If you choose your wording poorly, well, you understand, right?

And so, in Oprah's favorite verse the meaning of "delight" is important, because if you "delight" you shall rip back, as you will be provided *"the desires of your heart."*

I want to have all of my desires of my heart fulfilled! What did you say I should do? Oh, "delight myself in your Lord."

So where IS this Lord, this God? Everywhere. If we find DELIGHT all around us, then we are promised we'll be provided our desires.

That's cool. Let's keep with this line.

So, basically, we've said that instead of mere "gratitude" we should shift our consciousness to "Find pleasure in" or "take pleasure in" our lives. We've said that our wordings are important, and that they determine the quality of our lives. Actually, one of the great Roman emperors who ever lived, a person whose book is still revered nearly 2000 years later, Marcus Aurelius said that "The happiness of your life depends upon the quality of your thoughts."

So we are now trying to RAISE the quality of our thoughts, and thereby RAISE the quality of our life.

The wording of our thoughts is indeed important. There's a reason why we've encountered words as "Delight yourself" and "Desires of your heart", and "Pleasure". In fact, the original Hebrew word for the word "Delight" is equivalent to the word "Pleasure".

Therefore that verse from Proverbs can be read "Find PLEASURE" instead of 'delight' and you shall receive "the desires of your heart."

Now – let's look at these three words:

Delight, Pleasure, Desire

Is it only me or do they sound a little… inappropriate? A little… too… sensual?

I guess we live in a world in which everything that is passionate is deemed "wrong" and "improper", even if it has nothing to do with sexuality.

But words carry ENERGY and POWER.

I want YOU and I to begin using words that have HIGH energy and power attached to them. It's no coincidence that Oprah speaks of Pleasure, and that the most successful people speak of passion and pleasure ALL the time.

You may say, "Well, when I get a passionate life, I will speak with passion and pleasure." But my love, we know it's the other way around. You and I must be more daring, throw away much of our faded, dull, vague, energy-less blah-words such as "OK" and "fine".

"How was your day? Oh, fine."

Yuck! "How was your life? Oh, fine."

I don't want to have an OK-fine life. I wanna find Pleasure in life, and through being pleasure-prone, to show love to myself, to my life. It's simple. We need to AMPLIFY our wording, so we can AMPLIFY our love to life.

And that's what all the super successful people DO.

"I find my greatest pleasure, and so my reward, in the work that precedes what the world calls success."

— Thomas Edison
American inventor and businessman

"I find pleasure in everything - if I'm in a flea market, I'm there on my downtime, but I'm also there searching for the collection. I don't separate the two."

—Francisco Costa
Brazilian fashion designer

COLLECTING YOUR JOYS

So we looked into the importance of our words. And we offered to amplify our words. We also profoundly looked at the word "Gratitude" and how it stems from the root of "bringing pleasure". We therefore offered to look at "Pleasure" as our guide, rather than "gratitude". Now we'll look into embedding a culture of pleasure into our life.

How does that sound: "embedding a culture of pleasure into my life."

Does that sound good?

Or do you still have some residue of judgment and puritan criticism: "life isn't about having pleasure, it's about hard work!"

So what is this "pleasure" that I elaborate about so much, and why is it SO important?

Pleasure is one of my favorite words. Want to hear of some other favorite words?

Delight, Enchantment, Glee, Gratification Exultation, Exhilaration, Elation, Bliss…

These are just a few.

Shifting your consciousness to LIVING these words can be a very GRATIFYING thing indeed.

There are many ways of shifting one's awareness. But the easiest and most profound way is through everyday REFLECTION.

See, if I called you each evening, and we spoke for say, five minutes, and I'd ask you to tell me "what did you find pleasure in today?" the conversation might go like this:

"Pleasure?" you may say.

"Yep. Pleasure. What did you take pleasure in today, what brought you delight?"

"I…" you may hesitate, "I had a pretty good day, now, let's see, what brought me pleasure…"

"Or delight."

"Yes. Well…"

The first few days would be rather odd. You'd be finishing most of your sentences with an upward tone, like, "I guess my friend Brian called, and it was nice…?"

But after few weeks of me calling you EVERY evening, you will be quicker. Faster. "Oh, and also, I heard this great song I love on the radio… and I bought this new book just as a present to myself… and also- "

If I keep nagging you and calling you every single day, after few months you'd begin to see that your WHOLE life changed. The changed might have been subtle, but there was definitely a change.

When you get USED to it, you begin NOTICING things differently. Something good happens and you immediately say: "Oh, remember this for the evening call!"

When this happens, it means that your brain shifted to WANTING to remember the good. You will FOCUS on what works, what's good, what's pleasurable, what brings you delight. And we all know that what you FOCUS on, EXPANDS.

When I focus on my wife Hallel's lack of good mood recently, I might get agitated about that. I might comment to her that she is a little snappy recently. This is likely to bring to even more unhappiness from her, and a feeling that I criticize her. What will expand in this case is her *un*happiness.

Now, if instead, after I notice that she's in not so good mood lately, and I choose to FOCUS on the small things in which she IS in good mood, then I might enjoy seeing her when she nevertheless seems happy, and comment about that. That might bring us closer, it might open her up, we might talk, and slowly her happiness will EXPAND.

What we focus on EXPANDS. If we focus on "I don't have enough time" we'll get more of not having enough time. If we focus on "I have more than enough time for what really matters" we'll end up having more than enough time for what matters. This is simple, we ALL know it.

And, similarly, if we FOCUS on what brings us pleasure and delight, it will in turn EXPAND in our life.

I'm willing to bet you on that. On money, actually.

So, while I criticized the negative aspects of "Gratitude" (it feels like another SHOULD, you are EXPECTED to give thanks, etc.) I nevertheless support the actual GENUINE PRACTICE of gratitude.

We spoke about the power of questions in designing our life. Coach Tony Robbins says that quality questions lead to a quality life. Nobel Prize Laureate, Egyptian author Naguib Mahfouz has a wonderful quote I love:

"You can tell whether a man is clever by his answers. You can tell whether a man is wise by his questions."

Mahfouz puts the emphasis not on the answers we give, but on our questions.

I want to challenge you to ask a question each evening, and it should NOT be 'what am I grateful for?'

Instead, the question should be:

"What did I find pleasure in? What delighted me today?"

And be quiet. Hold the space. In the beginning you will HATE this question, as it speaks in a FOREIGN language. Most people speak "spoken OKnese",

"FINEish", "Common NOT-BADian".

Most people don't speak the "Rare PLEASUREish" and "Dialectic DELIGHTian". Actually, most people squirm when they hear people speak that way. They may say, "What happened to HER?!" or "Someone took a WOO-WOO pill!!!"

Yep. People don't SPEAK this language around you. But don't be upset with them. Begin, and they will follow too.

One hundred years ago there was a crazy guy called Ben-Yehuda, who sought to revive the dead Hebrew language, and use it as a modern language to unite Jewish immigrants to the Holy Land. Everyone laughed at him, and eggs were thrown at him. But years proved him right, and now modern Hebrew is spoken by millions.

I'm asking you to adopt a NEW language. This new language will in turn create a NEW outlook. The theory of Linguistic Relativity shows clearly that the structure of a language affects its speakers' cognition and world view.

I invite you, strongly, to enter a new chapter in your life, to learn the language of PLEASURE and DELIGHT through daily lessons.

Each day, write three things you took pleasure in or found delight in. It can be really powerful.

One thing I should note, though: this should NEVER feel like a chore. If you don't want to write, doodle instead. Draw hearts. Whatever suits you best that day. But keep the habit: it can take you only few minutes, and those few minutes can change your WHOLE outlook, and you life :)

"It isn't the great big pleasures that count the most; it's making a great deal out of the little ones"

—Jean Webster
American writer and author

"People often say that motivation doesn't last. Well, neither does bathing - that's why we recommend it daily."

—Zig Ziglar
American author and motivational speaker

PRACTICING SELF-LOVE

We managed to cram a lot into this little book, didn't we? Let's review some of the things we mentioned.

We mentioned the exercise I do each night in front of the mirror, speaking good words to myself, and at the end - hugging myself. Does that sound like something you might considering doing?

We spoke about putting yourself first. Constantly asking yourself, "But what do I want?" and then doing just that.

We spoke about not giving from what you don't have, meaning, to first give yourself, so that then you can overflow with love, and give others from that overflow, rather than from your own cup.

We did an exercise in which I spoke to your subconciousness, encouraging your inner self. It may have felt odd, but it came from a very sincere place.

We spoke of not caring too much what other

people say (remember? What other people say or think of you is none of your business!), but following your own heart.

We spoke about not running around doing things for other people all the time, of how my father prefers being abroad because he exhausts himself pleasing others. We spoke of how cellphones shouldn't be allowed in the bedroom.

We spoke about practicing the word "no" and saying it once a day, or at least once a week - learning to set your boundaries.

We did this exercise of "If I truly loved myself, I would…" and I encouraged you to THINK what would you do differently in your life. Now write it all down, and begin seeing to it!

We spoke of your duty to give the word a GREAT example of how to TREAT you. And you need to give us all a good example!

We spoke of not postponing your happiness "until", and giving it to you RIGHT NOW. No accomplishment in the future will change your self-love habits. Let me promise you that.

I asked you, "if today was your last day on earth, will you treat yourself the same way?" I wonder what did you answer. I wonder what are you answering right now.

We spoke of how we should treat ourselves like stars, and I did a little game with you, asking you "why is it cool to be you?" and we answered, you and I. I do hope that you participated, if not, I'll give you only one more chance when you reread this book. Otherwise I'm not playing again!

We spoke of how we should not use our "stories" to keep us stuck in our lives. Rather, I gave you an example of how I strive to see my story, with difficult moments in my childhood, as something that served me in making me more sensitive and aware. I encourage you to look into your story that same way.

This led us to speak of forgiveness. I did this elaborate exercise in front of you on how to forgive my former acting teacher, Jacob. It was powerful. Few days ago I thought of him again, and my emotions were not nearly as strong. I advised you to do the same process with someone you are angry with, not for THEM, but for YOU. You can do it in any way you wish, most people choose to do it in a letter, without any obligation to ever send it. It's for YOU, do whatever works for you, but liberate yourself from carrying the burden of anger. It's not good for you.

Then we took getting rid of our baggage to another level: getting rid of our secrets. Whether by telling a secret about our past or present to a trustworthy person, or through writing it down, we need to let go of our secrets. We spoke of how a research showed that keeping a secret makes you feel weighed down — literally — and even limits your ability to get things done.

We spoke of smiling yourself in the mirror. At least not just examining yourself so critically without at least LEAVING with a smile. That's unfair to the child inside you!

Then we spoke at length about adoring your body. I did a whole long exercise with you, describing how I acknowledge my forehead, my eyebrows, my nose... I encouraged and still encourage you to do the same!

Then we spoke of some "extreme" measures. I told you how I wrote a long love letter to myself; I told you how I wrote a love poem to myself; how I hung pictures of me as a child all around my office. How I took that one step forward and hung ALL KINDS of things, from diplomas, thank you letters, fun emails, greeting cards, memorabilia and other things that make me feel love to myself.

I offered you to do the same, and to also consider creating a PowerPoint presentation or a designated folder in your smart phone, in which you save all your screenshots, and you make sure to capture empowering moments (for example, whenever I receive a warm SMS from someone, I take a screenshot; whenever I see ANYTHING I like either on my lap top or my smartphone I capture it for my memory to be reminded over and over of the good stuff).

Then we took a necessary detour and we spoke about our inner psyche. That's when I brought up the three Self's (remember which three?) and their King. We spoke about how they work. This is a part of the book I'd recommend reading again and again, very often, so that you will be able to start exposing your self deprecating mechanisms, call them for who and what they are, and instead listen to your Intuition - who will tell you its all BULL and ask you to practice self love (she'll also tell you EXACTLY what you need to do. She's brilliant!).

That part is uneasy to some people. But practice does bring improvement (no perfection - we're throwing that word out!). So practice!

We then spoke of gratitude, it's Latin root, and how we should think of PLEASURE instead. I encouraged you to AMPLIFY your words, include more words such as "delight", "pleasure", "bliss", while I warned you, BEWARE of such words as OK, not-bad, fine - your life is a collection of your days. Make sure your days are filled with pleasure and delight over the little things, and so will your life be one of pleasure and delight.

As you can see, we covered LOTS of things in this little book. I see it as a little treasure, to which I packed, day by day, week by week, more and more ideas and personal stories in order to encourage YOU (and nobody else!) to begin PRACTICING the art of loving yourself.

The only question is: are you willing?

"Ask yourself the secret of your success. Listen to your answer, and practice it."

—Richard Bach
American author and aviator

"Practice yourself, for heaven's sake, in little things, and then proceed to greater."

—Epictetus
Greek philosopher and former slave

PRACTICING NEVERTHELESS

We just went through a short summary of what we covered in this book. The question now is, whether this book will be yet another nice read in your self-help, becoming a shelf-help rather than a true self-help – helping the books on your shelf rather than your own wellbeing?

I'm going to be a little bit in your face this chapter. Please forgive me, but I'm doing this FOR you.

We covered so much good in this book. Not because of ME as a writer, but because of the timeless principles it presented.

But for me, it will be a mere insult if you just move on without at least committing to two things you learnt in this book. Otherwise, my effort would feel to me a vain one. All of my honesty, my genuine and sincere interest in your success, in your ever-increasing self love, will be in vain.

You see, there's a reason why I mentioned below the previous quote the fact the author of the quote was an ex-slave.

Epictetus was a guy that was born a slave, and yet through education he was able to liberate himself and become a great philosopher. His philosophy helped countless of people. Especially, it helped convicts and prisoners throw their old habits of self-sabotage, and become truly free. For example, James Stockdale, an American fighter pilot who became a prisoner of war during the Vietnam War, credited Epictetus with helping him endure seven and a half years in a North Vietnamese military prison—including torture—and four years in solitary confinement.

Personally, I'm an amateur when it comes to Epictetus, but I do feel very close to him when I hear him say: "Practice yourself, for heaven's sake, in little things, and then proceed to greater."

I almost see him nodding his hand from side to side in disapproval, saying, "for heaven's sake, what's good in reading Jonathan's book if you aren't willing to practice the little things?"

I feel that we often run in life after great promises. Surely I've done so for many years, and I still fall into this trap now and then. I love self-help books. I long for the feeling of hope that I get in a beginning of book. I love the feeling of optimism that I have when I end it.

But I have learnt that I need to take PRACTICAL things and INCORPORATE them into my life, if I want to see ANY change.

And so I want to challenge you:

Will you commit to speaking yourself fondly in front of the mirror, and to writing three things that brought you pleasure each day?

Will you commit to hanging up pictures from your childhood, looking at them every day, while also taking two minutes each day to listen to your Intuition?

Will you commit to saying one 'no' each week, celebrating it and writing it as a success in a victory log you'll keep by your bed; will you also commit to writing a poem of love to yourself?

Will you be willing to commit to taking half a day once a month, to process the forgiveness process in your mind, and forgiving four people who you feel resentment for? Will you also commit to read two or three pages in this book every day in the next six months?

Will you commit to capturing screenshots of things that bring you joy, and looking through the folder once a day for few minutes on your smartphone or computer? Will you smile to yourself each and every time you pass by a mirror or a window, for at least five seconds?

Will you do the body acknowledgement exercise, going through each part of your body and expressing love, gratitude and apologizing for your judgment – once every three months? Will you ask yourself each day at lunch, "If this was my last day, will I be treating myself the same way?"

Will you commit to a moment of privacy each day,

or half a day of privacy each week? Will you not allow cellphones in the bedroom?

Will you commit to reading to yourself the chapter I wrote for your subconciousness, each day, until you will replace it with your own?

Will you commit to never saying "Yes" but instead, "Can I get back to you on that tomorrow"? Will you play the "I'm cool because" game once a day for 30 days?

Will you sit down to rewrite your life's story – and to find out all the reasons why that dark stain is actually serving you today? Will you commit to reading the chapters about letting go of your secrets, and read it each day for however long it takes till you get the courage to confide in someone or to write your secret down?

My question to you is: what will you commit to?

Write to me: j@kis-lev.com

I want to hear what are YOU committed to.

"If you deny yourself commitment, what can you do with your life?"

—Harvey Fierstein
American actor and playwright

"Life isn't about finding yourself. Life is about creating yourself."

—George Bernard Shaw
Irish playwright, critic and polemicist

RECREATING YOURSELF

I did MEAN it. Write to me. I WANT you to commit. I want you to improve your life. More than anything, I want you to improve your relationship with yourself.

We have this belief that we are who we are, "that's the way I am."

We see ourselves as a finished sculpture.

Let's look at that for a moment.

I studied sculpting in art school, and learnt a lot about working with clay. This is relevant to us as human beings, as many many ancient traditions compared the human being to clay. Even the Bible states, "We are the clay, , you are the potter" (Isaiah 64:8), and some translations translate the Hebrew word of "dust" to "clay", implying that instead of reading Genesis 3:19 as: "for dust you are..." we should read instead "for CLAY you are and to CLAY you will return."

Now, clay, I learnt in art school, and you probably

know it too, is never really 'done' until you burn it. It may SEEM hard as a rock. It may FEEL unchangeable. But unless it has been burnt, it is still SHAPABLE.

Now, to rescue an old piece of clay that you want to reshape, you need to soak it in tons of water, while giving it also lots of air (cause yucky fumes come out). You want to give it some time to really soak up the water.

After a while it gets tid bit softer, and it's time for you to start pressing on it, molding it with your hands, until it becomes softer, then you can begin really remolding it, and it's easy to work with, it's like butter!

Most of us, as people, think of us as a finished burnt product. Yet we are NEVER burnt. We can always remold ourselves.

What you just did, through reading this book, is to soak yourself up in water. Was it enough? Only you can tell. Some people need to read this book few tens of times before they get a little 'softer' so that they can start 'remolding' themselves. They might feel, as potters call it, that they are 'bone-dry' and that they need to soak more. "Soaking" can be reading and rereading, taking notes, highlighting, whatever wraps your mind around the information and energy in this book.

In the beginning, when you try to use your mental hands and mold yourself into the more self-loving person you want to become, you will find while you are softer, you are not yet malleable. Potters call it 'leather hard' – when the clay needs more movement, to be molded with your hands again and again, while making sure it has enough moisture.

This is what the practice is for. Each time you repeat your habit of self-love, you are making yourself more flexible. I promise you that with time you WILL become really easily molded into the person you want to be. Add some 'water' and 'moisture' on your hands by reading this book again and again, and steeping yourself in the quotes, in a moment we'll speak about the importance of the quotes. But basically, remember that each month you keep up with your daily habit, you are becoming softer.

After a long period of time, it may be months or even years, you'll find that you are UNRECOGNIZABLE. Oh yes. That's when you look at yourself, at your sweet loving self, at the person who is so self-loving and self-nurturing, and you don't recognize yourself. That's when you have become so 'plastic' or 'malleable'. You have designed yourself according to YOUR mental and spiritual hands, rather than according to your LIFE's circumstances.

That's when you participate in the divine CREATION. That's when you are closest to God, to the FLOW of the universe. That's when you ARE love, and you ARE joy.

Sure, you will harden at times. You will need more water, more inspiration, new habits or revitalizing your old ones. But still, you will be a different person. A person to YOUR liking, to YOUR design. And that is BLISS.

"You have to create your life. You have to carve it, like a sculpture."

—William Shatner
Canadian actor, director and author

"It's never too late to be who you might have been."

—George Eliot
19th century English novelist and poet

STEEPING YOURSELF

I KNOW that you can change yourself, change your life. I did it myself, and I keep doing it.

I remember sitting once in a lecture, and the lecturer said, "These days I don't have that negative inner chatter anymore. It took many years of work, but it's pretty much gone. Now it's mostly positive talk that I have inside, with only the occasional lapses, you know…"

I remember how hearing the lecturer made my heart feel. It's as if the words were like a beacon of light for my darkened heart.

At the time I was not believing my feeling of being not worthy of love will ever go away.

At the time I thought I needed to EARN someone's love.

And that included myself. For me to be nice to myself, I had to work really hard, achieve extraordinary things, and then I might get a pat on the shoulder from myself.

My self-talk was one that I do not wish for anyone to have. It was NEGATIVE.

Sure, from the outside you might have thought that I have it altogether. I was a young artist, making a living from his art in his mid-20s. Not bad. But I was in an unhealthy romantic relationship, which resembled all too much the relationship I had just left.

Intellectually I THOUGHT that I should be deserving of love and appreciation. But I didn't FEEL it, you know?

I remember once, how someone said that every baby deserves to be loved.

And my inner voice objected. ANY baby?? Really? What if... Well, what if...—

I couldn't come up with a sufficient excuse why a baby shouldn't be loved, but inside I felt like I – me – I was THAT baby, the one who shouldn't be loved.

It's hard for me to write these words. In fact these might be the most personal words I shared with you, and I think I shared some personal words with you. But this, well, I don't remember telling about it to anyone, really.

My self-talk was leading me to depression, to unhappiness, to constant work. I used to overwork myself, exhaust myself.

At this time of insufficient sleeping, of negative inner-attitude, I began to have awful back pains.

I cleaned the bathroom in a shared studio I was

renting, it was my turn. I had to head somewhere immediately afterwards, and I was in a rush. All of a sudden I felt an enormous pain, and found myself unable to keep standing. I fell to the floor.

This marked the beginning of some three years of horrific lower-back-pain. It would paralyze me for days, sometimes for weeks. When it did, I had to lean on the wall going from my bed to the bathroom and back.

At the time my body was signaling to me something I didn't want to hear. My body was saying: "SLOW DOWN!" and also "BE KIND TO YOURSELF!"

But all I was hearing was a distant echo, passing through thick forests of self-loathing and self-criticism. Was there self-hatred there too? Probably.

And Intuition, my lovely Intuition, she was nowhere to be found. I didn't know how to listen to her.

They say that when it rains it pours. I was in the second romantic relationship that had some elements of... abuse.

Why am I censoring my words? Guess I'm afraid of your judgment. The truth is that it was filled with elements of abuse. And so was the previous relationship. I just couldn't attract a good relationship to my life.

My business was going well, but I had to sweat for it. It didn't come easily.

And every few months I would find myself doing

some movement, whether it is closing the baggage door of the bus, carrying paintings from place to place – and all of a sudden a huge pain would attack me, and I would be paralyzed for a week, going to my parents' home or staying and lamenting my poor fate in my shared apartment, living with an incommunicative roommate I couldn't talk too, who left his dishes in the sink till they piled and I had to beg him not to do it again. And he did.

So, my self-talk, my self-esteem, my self-love - were at a low moment. I was on the fast track to long term unhappiness.

And what hurt the most was the relationship, feeling unloved and unaccepted for who I was.

Oh my God, it's SOOO hard for me to even recall this time in my life.

But something within me caused me to change. I began going to a shrink (I mentioned that earlier). I also began reading Chicken Soup for the Soul again. I liked these books.

In my late teens I read a couple of them, and loved them. But when my girlfriend then found out I read them, she laughed at me.

I then put them aside. When it came time to pack in Canada and go back to Israel, I left the book outside the suitcase.

But in my mid-20s, with a new girlfriend, I began reading this book again, and others in the series. And I watched some lectures by this Jack Canfield guy, who co-wrote these books. I liked him. He seemed so… gentle and genuine.

In one of his interviews he told about a workshop he did each summer, of one week long. He said it falls each year on his birthday, and that he loves celebrating his birthday that way, while being in a workshop setting encouraging people to go for their dreams.

I liked the fact he did that on his BIRTHDAY. And so, I began looking online for details.

And I signed up.

I haven't been to the States for several years, and the flights and the hotel costs were pretty high. But I said, "This is for myself."

In that one workshop I felt… as if I returned home. I cried a lot. I laughed a lot. I danced, I hugged, I felt at home. Better than the 'home' I knew. Real HOME. Like I could be MYSELF.

I hurried to sign up for a year long training with Canfield. It included four separate one-week-long workshops with him, and then I'd be a certified trainer, a sort of a coach.

Should I sign? I didn't want to be a trainer. But I LOVED the work. And Jack proved to be very genuine and loving.

I committed to a program that cost me basically all of my savings, and more. "This," I said to myself, "is for ME."

The next year I kept flying every few months to California for another workshop. One time, few days before the workshop, I was working hard to prepare few paintings before my 10 days away, when suddenly my back went out again.

Laying in my bed for the third day, with the flight approaching, I couldn't imagine not going. I hurriedly tried two different physical therapies that didn't work.

I called the airport and the airline, and arranged for a wheelchair to be ready for me in the three airports.

Being taken around on a wheelchair in a crowded airport, at the age of 26, felt a little unnerving. What made me a handicap? Well, I guess the way I overworked myself? It felt dumb. I felt stupid, and that nourished even more my cycle of self-loathing.

But I GOT there. Seeing the people I came to call my new friends, people committed to self-growth, made me extremely happy, and made my pain ease a little. I nevertheless had to lay on the carpet whenever my back was unwilling to keep sitting on the chair.

In between each workshop we had to have a sort of a coaching talk in small groups on Skype once or twice a week. That's when I was advised to begin saying 'no' to some of my obligations.

Also, it was in that time that I realized, painfully as it was, that my romantic relationship AGAIN was not working. Though I tried to put my everything into the relationship, I had to end it.

Months later, surfing on dating sites, I began writing love letters to myself, and trying to treat myself in the way I wanted others to treat me.

I then met Hallel. And I felt like my life were going in a better direction.

Each year since then seems to be better than the last. I'm still not where I want to be – I want to reach a stage in which my self-talk is extremely positive. I want to care less and less what others think. I want to be out there, in the world, doing and saying and standing for what I believe in, even though some people won't like my opinions. I feel that I have so much that I want to give the world, and I hope to find myself each year feeling more and more confident.

But I must say that where I am today is a miracle in comparison to where I've been. I used to have other people manage me. I used to feel torn between trying to please this gallery owner, that non-profit I was volunteering for, my parents, siblings, friends, girlfriend – I used to be so... unclear as to what *I* wanted.

These days I feel like I HAVE myself. Like I'm here for ME. Like my job is to ultimately make ME happy first, and only then the others. Others being my wife, my beautiful baby girl – I cannot give them from what I don't have myself. I therefore am constantly aware as to when I need time for myself, when I need a vacation on my own, when I need to be away from the cellphone for few hours, walking in the woods, dancing in my office, writing in my diary...

I take time for ME. I say NO quite often. I tell the

truth even when I know the other side won't be happy with me. I took my parents and I to a therapy, and we're working on things. They are very brave.

I tell Hallel when something she says or does doesn't feel pleasant for me. We talk. Real TALKING, I feel that she truly SEES me, you know? She's one of the greatest encouragements in my life, possibly the greatest after my own inner super-manly cheerleader ;)

These days I hug our baby girl, six-months old Sarah, a lot. In fact, she is laying on the carpet next to me right now, as I write. A Karen Drucker song, "I'm Gentle With Myself is played on repeat on my computer. It's midmorning, summer in the Galilee, and the sun is bright through the window.

I look at Sarah and I think that she is gorgeous. I do think that every child needs to be fully and wholly loved. And yes, without conditions, without prerequisites. Having her makes me understand how I should treat myself. Karen Drucker's voice sings, "I will only go as fast as the slowest part of me feels safe to go."

And I find these words wise. "I will be easy on myself, and I'll love myself like a newborn baby child."

I realize today that my parents, my grandparents, my siblings, my teachers, everyone around me did the best they could. And I realize that I needed more. Now I'm giving it to myself.

"Create the kind of self that you will be happy to live with all your life. Make the most of yourself by fanning the tiny, inner sparks of possibility into flames of achievement."

—— Golda Meir
Fourth Prime Minister of Israel

"Beauty is when you can appreciate yourself. When you love yourself, that's when you're most beautiful."

— Zoe Kravitz
American actress, singer and model

FAREWELL

I do hope that you enjoyed reading this book. I surely enjoyed writing it and conversing with you in my mind. I'd love to receive feedback from you. Please feel free to email me at: j@kis-lev.com

I highly recommend you to cut out the pages of the quotes and hang them up where you can see them. They were designed so that they will be esthetically pleasing, and I do hope that they bring lot's of joy to your life, and direct you in the direction you wish to go. No, I don't think it's bad to cut out pages from this book. It was designed so that you could cut the pages out. I want this book and its message to stick out with you for many years to come.

If you enjoyed this book, I would highly appreciate you rating it positively on Amazon, it only takes a minute.

ACKNOWLEDGEMENTS

I would like to express my gratitude to the many people who saw me through this book; to all those who provided support, talked things over, read, wrote, offered comments, allowed me to quote their remarks and assisted in the editing, proofreading and design. Tania von-Ljeshk for the editing and the support; Doug Ellis Photography for making me look good (; Slava "Inkjet" Noh for the cover design; Susan Leibtag for the encouragement; Marie-Noëlle Bélanger-Lévesque for the support. This book could have not come to life without you.

I would like to thank my parents, Betty and Isaac, for their love and constant encouragement over the years. This book is a tribute to the education you have given me.

I would like to thank my family: Steve, for believing in me; Romi for your love; Yoav, for your praise; Moria, for your wisdom; Elinoy, for your encouragement; Yanush, for your brotherhood in all times; Ilana and Shlomo Harel who were like second parents to me; Rachel and Michael Cherkis and the whole loving Cherkis family. Tal, Shirya and Moshe Bar-Ness; Samantha Silverman and Cyndi Silverman – I am blessed to call you all family.

I would like to thank my teachers: Geoffrey and Lilian Tindyebwa for countless of hours of listening and support; Peter and Alison Gardner for believing in me and encouraging me along the way. Louise Guenther for whispering courage to my ear. To all of those who left their mark of love on my soul: Edna Ziv-Av, Rachel Abramovitch, Rina Baruch, Cynthia Mackenzie, Daniela Kraemer; Sherry and Bryan Crowther, Gita Baikovitz, Michal Pinkwasser, Shifra Milshtein, and Arthur Kogan.

I would like to thank my mentors: Jack Canfield, for showing me a new kind of manhood; Shuli Ziv, for always telling the truth; Carol Kline, for your unconditional love; Ilan Hasson for bringing light in dark times; Avi Ben-Simhon for believing in me early on; Dudu Gerstein for encouraging me along the way with a knowing smile; Uvik Pundak, for always being there for me. To all of the inspiring figures in my life: Dr. Deb Sandella, Dr. Khursheed Sethna, Dr. Holly King, Alissa Bickar, Bryan Mannion, Gloria Belendez Ramirez, Lotte Vesterli, Ather Alibahi, Rina Hafiz and Amy Cady

I would like to thank my heroes inspiring me from afar: Iyanla Vanzant for finding peace from broken pieces; Oprah Winfrey for always sharing what you know for sure; Joel Osteen for the inspiration; Les Brown for shooting for the moon; T. D. Jakes for showing perseverance; Elizabeth Gilbert for never ceasing; Glennon Doyle Melton for being a true warrior; Lizzie Velásquez for your beauty; Nick Vujicic for your devotion; Tyler Oakley for your authenticity; Sidney Poitier for teaching me to say 'no'; Neil Strauss for constantly seeking the Truth; and Whitney Thore for standing against shaming and also for doing *it* whichever way (;

To my inspiring peace warriors: Jean and Dr. Reed Holmes for adopting me into your nest while I was still a little chick; Sami Al Jundi and Jen Marlowe for the great inspiration and for bringing sunlight into my life!; Ian Knowles for teaching me how to walk my talk; Andrea Kross and the Kross family; Sarah Stooß and the Stooß family; Dina and Oded Gilad; Debbie Rimon Ansbacher; Lee Rimon and Yitshak De Lange, Riman Barakat, Cara Bereck, Michelle Gordon, Atheer Elobadi, Karym Barhum, Tom and Hind, Max Budovitch, Micah Hendler, Eliyahu Mcclean, Mark Gopin, Amer and Asmaa Merza, Tarek Kandakji, Adi Yekutieli, Adaya Utnik, Alisa Rubin Peled, Peter Berkowitz, Elliot Jager, Chaya Esther Pomeranz, David Keller, Anita Haviv-Horiner, Oded Rose, Idrees Mawassi, Dalia Bassa, Rutie Atzmon, Ronny Edry, Anat Marnin, Muhammad Elbou, Dana Wegman, Omer Golan, Vardi Kahana, Rakefet Enoch, Avi Deul, Robi Damelin, Khalil Bader, Eyal Naveh, Uri Ayalon, Yael Ben-Horin Naot, Yosef Avi Yair Engel, Noa Karmon, Sivan Shani and Anchinalo Salomon and all the members of the President Young Leaders' Forum – you inspire me!

To all of my Pearson friends and UWC friends – I feel honored to call you my family.

To all of my Esperanto family – to mia E-o familio! Mi amas vin!

To my friends: Sharona Kramer and the Kramer

family, Daniel Prag and the Prag family, Hila Bakman and the Bakman family, Netta Granit-Ohayon and the Granit family, Edna Zamir, Hani Oren June Moore, Judy Martorelli, Salah Assanoussi, Mimi Green, Divya Lalchandani, Tara Sirianni, Michelle Tessaro, Julia Darmon Abikzer, Pat Newman, Aleta and Faith Kelly, Ileana and Andrea Tarkan, Sari Cortes, Vanessa VandeNes-Parrish, Lisa Purcell-Rorick, Michael Mann, Jennifer Zorrilla, Yinon Tsarum, Judith and Stephan Beiner, Clifton McCracken, Bobbi and Yaki Vendriger, Gaby and Dr. Jacob Reiss, Abigail and Dan Chill, Ileana Bejarano, Saba Misaghian, Jana Morehouse, Carmen Braden, Amanda Leigh, Samuel Thrope, Amir Djalovski, Dvir Pariente, Chen Arad, Natan Voitenkov, Niki Kotsenko, Itai Froumin, Gadi BenMark, Uri Shafir, Kay Wilson, Daniel Beaudoin, Your constant encouragement is water to my inner garden. Thank you!

Last and not least: I beg forgiveness of all those who have been with me over the course of the years and whose names I have failed to mention.

Above all I want to thank my wife, Hallel, who supported and encouraged me in this magical journey. I love you!

OTHER JONATHAN KIS-LEV BOOKS

Readers have asked me to include a section at the end of the book and speak of my other books. This section is therefore dedicated to all of you, my readers.

I've always loved writing, since childhood. Writing as well as reading (can you guess I was a real nerd?). For me, books were a way to expand my world. To travel. To "wake up". In the little village I grew up in books were all I had. Television was okay. But books – they were magnificent…!

I therefore always wanted to be a writer. In my early twenties I won an encouraging prize from an Israeli magazine called *Bamahane* for a short story I wrote. Yet it was only in my late 20s that I felt inclined to write a whole book: I realized back then that much of the lessons which helped me in my life came from my own tradition, from Judaism, from the holidays, from customs and sayings, from my parents' and grandparents' wisdom.

I therefore sat down and wrote for over a year a book which I called "Chutzpah: Success Secrets from My Jewish Upbringing". This book is filled with stories, anecdotes and lessons from Judaism. I believe that it helps explain why the Jews, who comprise only a half of one percent of the world's population, receive some 20 percent of the Nobel Prizes. It has nothing to do with genes, but with a way of thinking about service, and purpose, and calling... It's a very personal book, I share much about my grandfather, what I learned in my Bar Mitzvah ceremony, what are the key lessons imparted to children in each holiday and how, in my opinion, they shape the children into adults who want to contribute to the world. The book is filled with many photos as well, covering 3000 years of Jewish thought – but doing so in a simple and captivating way. I'd love for you to read it.

I then proceeded to write a book about pain and loss and hope in the Middle East. Ever since age eleven I participated in numerous peace programs between Israelis and Palestinians. These personal encounters not only won me Arab friends but also taught me quite a few valuable lessons about peacemaking. It's an emotional book, which I guarantee will not only make you moved, but also make you *hopeful*. It portrays the movement for peace in both sides of the conflict, a movement about which you rarely hear in the news... This book is called "My

Quest For Peace: One Israeli's Journey from Hatred to Peacemaking" and I'm super proud of it.

One of the key ways for me to work for peace has been my art. Since my early 20s I was fortunate enough to be able to make a living from my art, painting large canvases and selling them in galleries around the world. Many artists have asked me over the years how come I was able to achieve that level of success with my art. Between you and me – it wasn't really my talent. There are artists who are *way* better than I am. It was instead a set of *values* which I adopted from several older artist mentors I found. These values and valuable lessons made me successful in a field which most people affiliate with starving and suffering and being poor. Right?

Over the years, I shared these valuable lessons with many artists – not only with painters, but also with musicians, writers, and anyone interested. This led me to writing my third book, which I called "Masterwork: a Guide to All Artists on Turning from Amateurs into Masters". It's a beautiful book, filled with inspiring quotes by the history's greatest artists. I speak a lot in that book about the importance of finding a mentor and how to find one, of how originality isn't important but authenticity is *crucial*, and why the old myth of money spoiling the quality of art simply has to be thrown out the window. Many artists have reported to me that this book was a *game changer* for them, and I'm honored each time I hear that. "Masterwork" is an ideal gift to anyone you know who is into the arts or wishes to take their hobby to the next level.

My fourth book was not really a book. It was a journal. As part of my daily habits, I tried for many years to write five things each day for which I was grateful. This led me to design a journal that I would love to write in myself: each page has a date written on top. Five small lines are laid out for you to just jot down five things for which you're grateful. But the cream of the cake is a small picture frame for you to doodle in for few seconds. Those few seconds of doodling, gives a rather fun thing to do at the end of the day. At the bottom of the page I put an inspiring quote by people such as Gandhi or Oprah Winfrey or Eleanor Roosevelt - different quotes each day. For me, it's the perfect way to close the day before going to bed.

I called this journal "Gratitude Doodle: The One Minute a Day that Can Change Your Life." In it, there are a few chapters about the importance of gratitude, and an explanation as to how to use the journal to get the most out of it. I'm proud to say that there are whole families using it, each person in the family having their own copy. My wife Hallel and I also write in ours daily. It's a neat thing. It's one of the best ways I know to turn your life around and become more positive and grateful for all the good we have and forget to notice.

Another key way with which I bring joy to my life is

affirmations. While for most of my adult life I doubted the benefits of reading out loud positive phrases, in recent years I nevertheless found that it... *works!* I compiled over two hundred of my favorite empowering affirmations, and designed a book that is the most aesthetically pleasing book I could have ever envisioned. Each affirmation is given its own unique botanical illustration (gorgeous!). Flowers, plants, and even birds and butterflies fill each page, and it's impossible to not feel tranquil when you read it.

This book is called "Better Thoughts, Better Life: Super Powerful Affirmations to Snap You Out of the Funk in Two Minutes or Less." In it I also thoroughly explain about how to rewire our minds. Research shows that most of our thoughts are negative. A trained mind can *shift* that. I am working on it myself, and I'm glad to report that due to using affirmations, my negative inner-chatter has dramatically subsided. I look at this book, "Better Thoughts, Better Life" as the best gift you can give *yourself*. It's simple, but true: when you improve your thoughts, you improve your life. That's what "Better Thoughts, Better Life" is all about.

I followed that book with a book about choosing happiness. Over the years I learned that in each and every moment I have a choice. A simple choice: I can either focus on what doesn't work, or on what brings me pleasure in that moment. It's a simple exercise that can be overlooked due to its simplicity. But it is as powerful as gravity. Every other moment during the day I shift my thoughts from negative to positive ones. This enables me to be happier, as well as makes me more motivated to achieve more in life. It's really powerful. I wrote a small book about this habit and how to acquire it, and called it "Every Other Moment: A Manual on Choosing Happiness". I love it. It's a great reminder about the power we have at each given moment to change our lives for the better.

Being a rather positive guy, over the years I encouraged many friends around me to go for their dreams, to get that ideal job, to ask for a raise, to create a side business. I noticed how many of my women friends had a harder time boasting about their abilities than my friends who are men. This puzzled me for many years, and it wasn't until the last five years, where I found myself with a highly capable woman as my partner, that I began questioning why is that. Why is that that women tend to be smarter than men (there's research to back this up) but at the same time don't toot their horns nearly as much? Why do women don't tend to negotiate their salaries like men do? And why do women attribute their success to luck while men attribute their success to their own doing?

This led me into writing a very emotional guide for women called "Brag Woman Brag!" This book is my gift to my wife, my mother, my daughter, my sisters, and all of my friends who happen to be women. I quote many researches showing how there is a negative bias toward girls who lead. Boys who lead are called 'strong', while girls who lead are called 'bossy'. I take the reader through a very profound emotional journey to rediscover their power. It's my gift to women. And even the most skeptic of women, who have disliked the title, the cover, and the whole idea, write to me back saying "Wow." I cried over reading some of the emails from readers of "Brag Woman Brag", simply because this book hits a nerve. I hope that in a few years it will become irrelevant. But for now, it is one of the most relevant topics each woman (and man) should explore. It's important for us ALL to own our power.

All of these books are available both electronically, as well as in print. You can find them easily online. Thank you for your support and interest!

Jonathan.

Notes

Notes

Notes

Notes

CONTACT

The author can be reached via e-mail at
KislevTV@gmail.com

Or on Facebook, Twitter and Instagram as:
KislevTV

ABOUT THE AUTHOR

Jonathan Kis-Lev is an Israeli peace activist, artist, a television personality and an author.

As a peace activist, Jonathan has been involved with several peace organizations in the Holy Land, beginning from age 11. In 2014 he co-founded the Hallelujah Dialogue Group in Jerusalem, along with Palestinian peace activist Riman Barakat.

As an artist, Kis-Lev developed his own unique style, dubbed as "Naïve Art". His paintings were shown in exhibitions around the world, most notably in Europe, Canada, and the United States. Kis-Lev also acted in numerous Israeli television shows, and co-hosted Israel's Balbalev Talk Show for teens.

As an author, Kis-Lev won the 2007 Bamahane Magazine Award for Short Story. He since then published five books: "Chutzpah: Success Secrets From My Jewish Upbringing"; "My Quest For Peace: One Israeli's Journey From Hatred To Peacemaking"; "Masterwork: A Guide To All Artists On Turning From Amateurs To Masters"; "Gratitude Doodle: The One Minute A Day That Can Change Your Life"; and "Better Thoughts Better Life: Super Powerful Affirmations To Snap You Out Of The Funk In Two Minutes Or Less".

Jonathan lives in Israel's Galilee, with his wife Hallel and their daughter Sarah. This is his ninth book.

69976697R00148

Made in the USA
Middletown, DE
10 April 2018